Tarot for Romeo and Juliet

CAMELIA ELIAS

Tarot for Romeo and Juliet

REFLECTIONS ON RELATIONSHIPS

Tarot for Romeo and Juliet:
Reflections on Relationships

© Camelia Elias 2021. Published by EyeCorner Press 2021. Denmark. Designed & typeset by Camelia Elias. Set in Fabiol and Rialto. Images: Carolus Zoya Marseille Tarot, ca. 1680 © Camelia Elias.

This book is published in three editions: a hardback edition limited to 193 copies bound in red silk, stamped in gold and gilt edges, red ribbon and mother of pearl, rosa end papers; signed by the author; printed and bound by Narayana Press on Munken Pure Rough 150 gsm paper; and two unlimited paperback and ebook editions.

PAPERBACK ISBN: 978-87-92633-81-1
EBOOK ISBN: 978-87-92633-83-5

All rights reserved. No part of this book may be reproduced in any form, without written permission from the publisher and the copyright holder.

www.eyecorner.press

For the woman who knows the heart of man

Contents

Counterpoint 10
Under the balcony 11

Punctuation sheet 22
The assurance of love 23

In love and war 32
Two cures for love 33

Romeo wants a drive 48
Juliet's armor 49

November 54
Juliet is 53 55

Conquest of the useless 62
The heart of man 63

Thinking with Demons 74
Return to passion 75

Hard rain 84
The cognac magician 85

The eleventh gate 96
Thresholds 97

Satisfaction 106
The Knights Templar 107

All that is more 116
Death on wheels 117

Redemption 134
'Give me my Romeo' 135

References 140
Acknowledgments 142

THE END AND THE MEANS (To desire something passionately means suppressing the heat of any other desire, means fusing all your desires into one, possessing nothing in order to claim everything at once. The most deprived have the maddest desires. Emptiness aspires to be filled. Wanting to be the poorest for love in order to be one day — who knows? — the most fortunate...)

— EDMOND JABÈS

Counterpoint

'I'm ready to be happily married,' Romeo says to his second Juliet, the first one having left him in counterpoint with time.

'Enter my world,' the second Juliet says, unaware of the rebound in counterpoint with love.

The cure for love is a greater love. This, every musical fugue knows, but if the second Juliet is illiterate she will not know that what she's about to receive is not Romeo's devotion but his death.

It is hysterical to think — also a contrapuntal state — that the only thing that can make this union work is watching vampire movies on a big screen.

The lovers at odds can dream of resurrection, while the first Juliet haunts their time beyond impalement. The greater love already happened, with her, in the first summoning of the night.

Under the balcony

HEARTS ON FIRE. FIRST HIM, THEN her. Romeo is under Juliet's balcony, talking about the moon that can't compare to the beloved. He is inflamed by visuals. She, by names. Romeo is her lover, but his name is her enemy. 'Call me but love, and I'll be new baptized' (Act 2 Sc. 2), he declares, after Juliet waxes philosophical on the nature of words. He envisions himself as the embodiment of the glove on her hand. What does it matter what such a glove is called? But Juliet knows better. You can't be messing with the names that seal your fate. Juliet knows the heart of man. The man knows love. What's the difference? I haven't seen others putting it quite this way, but I venture to say that, after some 400 years of Shakespeare analysis, this immortal drama about lovers who can't have one another is about knowing the difference between love and knowledge of hearts.

Contemporary filmmaker and script writer Werner Herzog has repeatedly said that you can't be a master at your craft, unless you know the heart of man. But how do you do that?

While Herzog hardly elaborates on what he means, if you pay attention to what else he says in the course of a sermon on filmmaking, you'll catch other phrases that give you an indication. In one of his public interviews he once mentioned that knowing the heart of man has to do with 'knowing the epicenter of their fears.' Fair enough. Although still on the intangible side, fear is more graspable than an unprocessed knowledge about it, as fear occurs on an intuitive plane prompted by projections. As with any projection, we're with a visual text, so to speak, as we can't fear anything unless our imagination kicks in, molded also by dramatic language and a particular set of words that conjures a mood. When we fear, we're with mood and atmosphere, rather than time and existential philosophy. What we want to know is not *when* we meet the monsters, but rather *how* we slay them in the fog.

If you read Shakespeare's play carefully, you'll notice that the way in which he sets up the drama relies very much on contrasting mood with time, or rather the contrapuntal in time against the background of weather. The protagonists can be in the mood for something, but if the weather forecast is bad, you can be sure that the tempest wins if the prediction is correct. In this sense we might call what Shakespeare does meteorology, or taking the temperature of how hot or cold the heart is when it faces vicissitudes. It's one thing to be passionate about what summer promises, and another to live through drought. The mood for love can quickly turn into a walk in the desert, the *fata morgana* illusion becoming Dracula's bride.

When Romeo and Juliet have their famous discourse under the balcony, what we instantly note is how each lover perceives the weather in their hearts. While Juliet's speech is about tactics towards avoiding the clashing winds between the Montagues and the Capulets, the two rivaling families, Romeo is less concerned. He is not into philosophizing. He is a man of action. He will happily renounce his name, if that is what the mistress of his heart wants. But is this a question about what the woman wants, to change the names as one would change the color of a power-point when the lecture goes stale and the audience is not paying attention any more? Changing the costume works for the uneducated audience, but what is underneath the cloth when validating the audience is not the aim?

I love it when Juliet insists on taking the temperature of language, with the barometer always showing preferment for the dominant. Thus she asks, waiting for an argument:

My ears have not yet drunk a hundred words
Of that tongue's utterance, yet I know the sound:
Art thou not Romeo, and a Montague? (2.2)

But none is given. No argument, as Romeo is an optimist:

Neither, fair saint, if either thee dislike. (2. 2)

The reader wants to blurt at him: 'what's wrong with you, man? Have you lost your mind? What has this woman's justified fear to do with likes and dislikes?' Juliet fears the wrath of her family and Romeo's family if they learned about this love, simply because she is better at reading the atmosphere between them. Why can't he? Enter Herzog, our modern day Shakespeare, giving us Isabelle Adjani and Klaus Kinski in the roles of Lucy and Count Dracula in the cult film *Nosferatu* from 1979. We're with Romeo and Juliet again, yet cast in deconstructed characters compared to what I'm talking about in the old Shakespearean context. 'Enter my world,' the vampire Romeo says to her, 'and your lover won't die.' Juliet/Lucy/Isabelle gives in and receives Dracula's death that is also her death, so that the other Romeo/Jonathan/Ganz can once more ride into the sunset in search of Juliet number two, or another number that gets to be multiplied all according to what the weather prescribes. In Herzog's film it's clear that this Juliet also knows the heart of man, the sublime occurring exactly at the moment when we notice a crossing of aims. Romeo in his thoughtful incarnation as Count Dracula is exactly on the same page as Juliet, the Luc(y)ferian light, insofar as they both know exactly what the deal with love is. The proper words then lead to the proper touch, and they die happily ever after.

Now, what has this got to do with the book you're reading? Everything and nothing. But consider the following. In the classic fortunetelling tradition there's no greater question than this one: 'does he love me?' I like this question, as there's no end to what it can disclose at the level of how we know the heart of man. When it comes to suffering from a heartache, both men and women experience the same intensity. We go from high enthusiasm under the balcony to fear and trembling that if it's good, the love, then it's too good to be true. It gets even more interesting when a third party is involved. The drama of rivalry and jealousy, possession and the burning secret that screams to get out are unmatched. As a fortuneteller you simply don't get the same excitement when all you have to address is a question about money, or how to deal with an imbecile boss.

In a contest between questions about love, work, money, and health, love runs with the medal. Relationship wins. Although the other type of common questions can be said to be equally as much about relationship (with your finances, colleagues, or your own physical and mental state), the love question has higher stakes, as you always run the risk of encountering your own naked heart when you pose it. This is dangerous business. It may explain why, actually, it is more common than uncommon to answer questions about situations when the heart is only temporarily engaged, with commitments broken into half and even smaller measures. One may be committed to one's craft, wholeheartedly, but how often do we get to know the true heart at work, when the investment has a distant nature, being devoid of emotional intimacy? Not all are Pygmalion, in love with their own creation, the sculpted body of a goddess that deserves life through passionate kissing.

I don't get many questions about love these days, and I lament this situation. As a fortuneteller, I would prefer to see that we flung the cards in the face of the ones whose hearts are not up to speaking anymore, because it hurts so much. There's a lot in this suffering that makes us stay wide open towards the flying wisdom that comes our way in the encounter with a bleeding heart. While one can hurt quite badly and be anguished about a money situation, it's just not the same when it comes to knowing something about the heart itself when it is invested in the material, however seductive and full of promise this territory may be. What I want to see more of is not adrenaline, but its consequences, negotiating eloquence without insult given or injury taken.

When I get to tackle questions about love, especially the kind that renders lovers at odds with their fate, I come close to seeing what everyone is made of. I get to stick my own finger right into the epicenter of fear. And why is this? Because love, the high caliber type, is very rare. Its counterpart is the highly calibrated love, the measured love according to cultural standards of expectation: you get born, you fuck, and die. But in between these states there's the approximation of intimacy that leads us straight to knowing something about the heart. I read the cards for that.

In this book I start every chapter with a prose poem that features a staging of what we may term 'deconstructed lovers' in the image of Romeo and Juliet. How do we know the hearts of lovers, the hearts of all those who live intensely and without compromising the integrity of their honesty? Yet since honesty cannot always be communicated directly, it's not a given that we can read profoundly what moves the heart. We use cards to prognosticate the weather a soul is under. We take the temperature of the heart and strip it bare to its essential language, which is the language of justice.

But why is it interesting to look at *Romeo and Juliet* in the context of reading cards for relationships? Think about it. It's all about reading the signs accurately. Shakespeare sets an example of what happens when lovers, while being on the same page where love is concerned, are unable to communicate effectively towards living together. In their attempt to bypass their mutually hating families, Romeo and Juliet are constantly at odds with one another. There is a plot to fake a death and thus escape the old rivalry. First Juliet dies. Then because the message about her death not being a real one fails to reach Romeo, he dies. She wakes up after having ingested a 'temporary' poison, and when she sees him dead for real by her catafalque, she takes her own life. All this drama because the signs were misread and miscommunicated. How tragic is this? Very tragic. I can imagine what might have happened if they had consulted a fortuneteller about their predicament instead of the enterprising monk who prepared the poison for Juliet.

Formally, however, we get a hint from Shakespeare as to what the real tragedy is all about, beyond the world of plot and theme. Language. The careful reader will have noticed already in the first exchange that Romeo speaks a language that is not Juliet's. He is exuberant. She is exultant. Energy and excitement against the triumphant and the powerful. You would think that these two go together, but not necessarily. Excitement has to do with expectation. The triumphant has to do with realization. As we will see, Juliet is on this level, situating her love in the realm of the done deal. Meanwhile there's nothing Romeo wants more than to share Juliet's bedsheets. To begin with. But she is already beyond this phase. She makes this clear in how she frames her language about how she feels. Romeo can't follow her, but he is ready for what she proposes. He is in the mood for what she already consciously staged.

In the context of divination, when we read for moods we're beyond time; the time it takes some lovers to never forget their broken hearts, never move on, or re-instate themselves on rebounds, whether for the purpose of self-preservation or to cross the old lover. Every reading of the cards in such situations is a reading for 'the one and only' beyond cliché, for what we're dealing with here is an act of unconditional surrender that requires faith. What heart emerges from this faith? Can the fortuneteller refine the art of acceptance? Entice to surrendering to the reality of infinite love? Who gets to experience it? What do the cards say about *that* adrenaline?

Shakespeare's Romeo used his passion as a glove, racing like Ayrton Senna's hands on Juliet's thighs, his Formula One vehicle. Meanwhile, the words for her had the function of sharpening the ax. While Romeo was on speed, Juliet was strategizing. When she said to him, 'Thou know'st the mask of night is on my face' (2.2), she didn't offer this image as part of a cautionary tale. She offered it as a test. Romeo was right there, singing her praises under her balcony, but what was his spine made of? Could Romeo distinguish between the masks? He was quick to offer to swear that his love was more than shallow. 'What shall I swear by?' he asked her, to which she replied:

Do not swear at all;
Or, if thou wilt, swear by thy gracious self,
Which is the god of my idolatry,
And I'll believe thee. (2.2)

'O Romeo, Romeo? Are you sure of your words?' I want to ask in Juliet's voice, addressing the subtle language of silence, for how can one be sure of words? How vividly can one depict a name? Then say it loudly yet without saying it, so Juliet can hear it with her heart, one that can distinguish between the colors of the lover's tongue.

Let's get closer to this image by offering our fortunetelling veins to the meanest, and yet most romantic of vampires. If it's not to achieve the immortality of knowing the heart of man, then why read the cards at all?

UNDER THE WEATHER

'What went wrong?' A fair question, and a common one at that. A woman madly in love can lament the loss of her husband over what she perceives is nothing. 'I don't get it,' she says, looking hopefully to your hands, as you shuffle the cards. 'Everything was fine, and then everything was not fine anymore. And no, there *is* no other woman. I checked. Now he wants a divorce.' You keep shuffling the cards, looking for signs that may disclose what is unsaid, but eloquently present between the lines. Then you let three cards hit the table: the World, Death, and the Star.

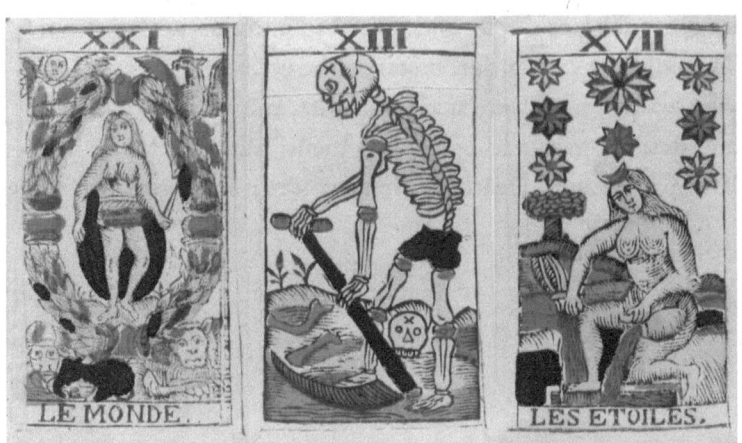

'Was there a woman in the past? you ask.

'Yes, but he got over her.'

'Are you sure about that? You yourself hold the promise of the world for him, but did he truly give you his love in return? What if what he gave you was his death, a pile of bones that the other one still worships? Why did you marry him? Because he said the words? Did you make him swear by his gracious self, the god of your idolatry that these words, *I love you*, were intended for you alone beyond any settled negotiation?'

Silence. Try to imagine the woman I was reading these cards for. Try to visualize her face in between each of the questions I asked her to consider. If you can feel the weight of this silence getting heavier and heavier after each question mark, then you get to know what I mean by reading for the heart, the storm in it battling the fire of its volcano.

The woman here didn't have an answer, as she was lacking the words. But her heart knew better. Sometimes 'the other woman' is not a new interest, but the past in the forever future. Sometimes the second Juliet can never outrank the first. Then divorce is in order. It settles the unending question of why — since vows were said — one that the heart both knows and desires against its better judgment. 'Why can't it be me?' 'Because it can't,' Death answers, 'you're not the one.'

Punctuation sheet

In times of scarcity what's pressing on our minds is hearing the unholy trinity speak:

Get paid, get laid, lose weight!

But what is the color of our tongues when we say 'I want' and in the process forget the proper punctuation for it?

'O Romeo, Romeo! wherefore art thou Romeo?' Juliet laments without the exclamation mark.

It's impossible to hold on to love when you never really know it.

'How about it?' the young nudge one another in a colorless voice, jumping in a boring bed that dreams in monochrome of starched and crumbled poplin sheets, white as the brightest star in a constellation near the knowing heart.

The assurance of love

IT IS CLEAR THAT THE LANGUAGE Shakespeare's Romeo speaks is much younger than that of Juliet. He has confidence in himself. She, in the cadence of her words. He speaks in clichés, the language of imitation. She, in the erotic idiom, the language of infinity. You'd think that because of his boldness, it's the other way around. But this is not so. The one in control of the erotic phenomenon is Juliet. In their exchange about the assurance of love, what Juliet puts on the table is the ultimate. Still under the balcony, when they reluctantly have to part, she first courteously bids him goodnight with these words:

> Good-night, good-night! as sweet repose and rest
> Come to thy heart as that within my breast! (2.2)

Upon Romeo's dismay, 'O, wilt thou leave me so unsatisfied?' demanding also that they exchange faithful vows, Juliet replies that she already gave hers before he even requested it, and that she would do it again. Then the sublime assurance:

> My bounty is as boundless as the sea,
> My love as deep; the more I give to thee,
> The more I have, for both are infinite. (2.2)

What did Romeo understand? Not much, but he did identify the unsettling mood in all things boundless, by calling the sound of the lovers' tongues 'silver-sweet' in response to Juliet's analogy:

> Bondage is hoarse, and may not speak aloud;
> Else would I tear the cave where Echo lies,
> And make her airy tongue more hoarse than mine,
> With repetition of my Romeo's name. (2.2)

Romeo's own visions of synesthesia, identifying colors in taste and taste in sound, echo Juliet's own projections of her heart's desire to love endlessly, and it is in this that they meet, that is to say, in the tongue natural to infinity.

THE STUPIDEST THING

Now imagine this transposed to a divination setting when what you often have to pay attention to is not only what the sitter says, or even what the cards show, but rather to what is not on the table. Lovers speaking in the tongue of infatuation, ardent passion and all the torment and anxiety that stems from that, do not always have Shakespeare's vocabulary at hand, when even clichés exhibit a particular scent and flavor. I'm interested in what is *not* said, in what remains unarticulated or expressed as a language of secrets, filled with suggestion, ambiguity, and ambivalence. So how do we read the cards when such a mood presents itself to us? What do we pay attention to? In a previous book, *What is Not: Marseille Tarot à la Carte* (2019), I offer the idea that when the reader is faced with gaps, what is best to do is pay attention to the eyes and the hands of the sitter. Then pay attention to all the eyes and the hands represented on the cards. What language do they speak? Does this language match the words to say it?

Once upon a time, lovers on the same page — yet sharing the same predicament that we can identify in Shakespeare's *Romeo and Juliet;* he using the language of pragmatism while she that of abstraction — presented me with this situation, though I didn't have both of them consulting me at the same time. The woman said this to me: 'I know he loves me, but why does he always have to say the stupidest thing to me? What are his real thoughts about me?' I love a classic question. Three cards fell on the table: the Devil, the World, and the Moon.

The Devil is a Lord of Darkness, matched only by the Moon, the Mistress of the Night. The World is all her own. I offered this thought: 'your lover says stupid things to you because he is intimidated by your perfect orchestrations. Your command has an elevated nature that he can't comprehend. And yet he is both attracted to it and fears it at the same time. There's nothing you can do about it. From your vantage point, although difficult, you *can* read the language that's beyond human vocalization. The Devil and his imps and the Moon and her dogs share the same dark territory. There's howling and gesturing. Learn this language, if you're to avoid confusion, or else bring the man to your own level. Teach him what you know.'

The deeper implications of this discourse is the realization that what these lovers need is to find a common ground that lends itself to a correct reading of one another's hearts. It's not enough to know that love is present. Romeo and Juliet also knew that their love was present. And yet they died a stupid death. What then?

Lovers need awareness that conflates space and place together through ways of seeing, or rather perceiving how they become part of one another. Just think about how the complexity of images — haptic, graphic, mental, verbal — created by what we imagine, project, and expect from one another is like a vortex of unfolding a force of movement. We move each other, if, when, and how we think of each other. Sometimes this thought materializes in specific acts: acts of courtesy, acts of goodness, acts of love. This is what touches. When words fail us, what touches us is an image, namely the image of seeing how we can suppress the heat of all our desires that are not already connected to the one and only aim in love, which is linked to understanding clearly the heart of the other.

In my reading above, what the cards also disclose is that although this woman's lover desires to understand her whole world — yet cannot — what he also wants is to possess summoning power. He wants to say to the woman, 'enter my world, and I'll show you what I'm capable of' — the domain of the Devil — but this woman has everything already. She has *the* world, and hence all the power. What else can he offer her? Occult knowledge, perhaps. The Devil together with the Moon pack a seductive punch, but would the woman who hovers above the ground *and* the underground be interested?

What emerges from this is the man's frustration expressed as 'the stupidest thing.' The pragmatic speech act infused by the exuberant desire to get satisfaction, 'how about it?' fails, especially when the man realizes that the woman he loves doesn't just dream of a bed dressed in starched poplin; she has one such already. Thus the question that I was interested in probing for my sitter was the extent to which she was aware that what she was up against was a dark force to be reckoned with, but one that at the same time was stunned, drowning in its own impressions. While she may have been able to mediate the man's desires against his projections, most of them false considering the moon's reflections, it was not so clear how the man's motivation could match her being beyond an agenda.

How could these people, then, assure one another intelligently of their love, the love that was present in its deeper cut, the cut that united the above and the below, heaven and hell? Time to bring in the philosophers.

THE EROTIC CALL

One of my favorite writers on the subject of love is philosopher and theologian Jean-Luc Marion, who has this to say in his seminal work *The Erotic Phenomenon* (2007). Allow me to quote at length here in the interest of getting beyond the surface of language.

> Only eternity responds to erotic reason's need for the assurance of the present – knowing definitely whom I love [...] 'Will I have the strength, the intelligence, and the time to love you to the end, without remainder or regret?' for the one that I love clearly imposes herself upon me as a saturated phenomenon, whose endless and measureless intuition does not cease to overflow all of the significations that I attempt to assign to her, beginning with the first among them, 'Here I am!' Seriously facing the face of the other, or more precisely, the face of this unsubstitutable other of whom I claim to be the lover, requires that I give without end a new meaning to the intuitions that never cease coming to me, and thus that I say all the words and pronounce all the names I am able to mobilize, or even that I invent others, so as to accomplish the indefinite interpretation. The lover never finishes telling himself of the beloved, telling himself to the beloved, and telling the beloved to herself. The lover, in front of the intuitions that the beloved inspires in him, must deploy an endless hermeneutic, a conversation without endpoint; thus he needs a period of time without bounds in order to carry out his discourse without conclusion. Love demands eternity because it can never finish telling itself the excess within it of intuition over signification. I will only know whom I love in the final instance – by eschatological anticipation of eternity, the sole condition of its endless erotic hermeneutic. Thus, only eternity answers the need of erotic reason

concerning the assurance of a future – being able endlessly to tell me whom I love and to make it known to her, since without me, she would not know it (Marion, 2007: 210).

If asked, Marion would say the same as The Beatles, 'all you need is love.' Perhaps this is so. But it seems that the continuity of love, insofar as it needs constant reassuring, is dependent on the incentive to give nothing to itself. How else to understand endlessness? Juliet understood her love precisely in terms of giving nothing to itself, but she elected to communicate this to Romeo by way of invoking the assurance of her infinite bounty: 'the more I give to thee, the more I have…' As reassurance comes in fragments of speech, it supplements continuity with 'everything' which is also 'nothing' at the same time. In other words, if the proposition 'all you need is love' is correct, then it can only be so if it runs counter to time as a matter of necessity. Thus we don't operate with either the past or the future, but with their assurance. Perhaps this is what Marion means to suggest when he further says the following:

> To love requires loving without being able or willing to wait any longer to love perfectly, definitely, and forever. Loving demands that the first time coincide with the last time (211).

Romeo and Juliet achieved this in their contrapuntal encounter with time. And yet, while their love coincided with eternity, their language failed the communication test. Romeo paid for his exuberance with Juliet's price for her triumph. She defeated her first death, but not the second. As Heraclitus said, 'you cannot step into the same river twice.'

THE DEVIL'S PASSION

Enter Romeo: 'she told me that I came up as the Devil in the reading you gave her. She told me what you said about me.' I squint at the man and ask, 'and?' 'Perhaps you hit a nerve,' he says. 'Perhaps? What do you mean by this tentative assurance, a limiting of your imagination?' I further probe, but Romeo doesn't answer me. 'I also want a reading,' he says instead, reaching nervously for my hand. He heard about the rule of crossing the fortuneteller's palm with silver. I'm going to charge him more, though, for my service. No one says, *perhaps* to me when they mean the opposite without paying extra for it. I don't transact with fear and its approximation.

Three cards fall on the table, and I start speaking in the man's voice, the voice of the Devil that he already brought to my parlor, now in dialogue with the fortuneteller, the I in the third person.

'What is the logic of this? This temptation I feel in my soul?' the Hermit, looking at Justice, wants to know. The High Priestess goes, 'there's no logic. Because it's in the soul.'

'Am I the Hermit, then?' Romeo wants to know, and I urge him to answer that question himself. But what kind of a lover is he? What did Marion just say? Let's have that again:

> The lover, in front of the intuitions that the beloved inspires in him, must deploy an endless hermeneutic, a conversation without endpoint; thus he needs a period of time without bounds in order to carry out his discourse without conclusion (210).

I ask the man: 'are you looking for a conclusion or for understanding? Some understandings are inconclusive. Are you ready for those?' As a skeptical Hermit invested in doing methodical work, he is looking for his true justice. But how can he find it, if his approach is one whose premise is indirect, paved with 'perhaps' and 'maybe' and the ultimate arrogance: 'why should I give you the satisfaction of admitting that you are right about me?'

What this Romeo didn't count on is the fact that this fortuneteller is not wasting her time. I told him to look for the law of insufficient reason. If he could formalize for that, he would be able to approach his lover with more than magnetic apprehension. 'For it is written,' says the High Priestess, 'that if you seek Justice with a lamp and a cane, Justice will give you in return a sword and a scale.'

In love and war

In the open the Montagues and Capulets make declarations of war. In secret they make declarations of love. The secret wins. It has more mojo.

'I can't make you part of my world, and declare my love to you,' Romeo says to Juliet, 'because you're already taken.'

This Romeo sounds like Confucius interpreting the **I Ching**: 'now is not the time to act; proceed slowly. Obstructions ahead.'

Meanwhile Juliet goes: 'wise, wise... and yet, my bounty is as boundless as the sea, my love as deep.'

What law governs the secret that fears a mistake? A waiting strategy is a winning strategy, if and only if Romeo takes a dive into Juliet's mirrors.

Two cures for love

SOMETIMES OUR MOST BRILLIANT turns of phrase are not ours at all. Remember the line in the first poem here, 'the cure for love is a greater love?' I took credit for it because this line was gifted to me by my best friend. So it's mine. But it didn't originate with me. 'You can have it,' the man said, when I prophesied that it won't be long before I was going to need it. That is to say, *need it* in that form that claims complete possessiveness and authorial force over the thought of another. Anthony W. Johnson, professor of Renaissance studies, musician, and Shakespearian scholar once told me about his greatest love. One that remains unmatched to this day. This happened in Turku, in Finland, more than a decade ago, when I was on research leave from my university in Roskilde in Denmark. I had permission to step into the occult Steiner Library and read some books. In my application to visit, a visit facilitated by my colleague and friend, I didn't mention any potential pacts with Devils that I might also make, in addition to merely reading about them. I followed the appropriate rules of conduct, and all was fine, but there was nothing that prevented me from using whatever knowledge I came across and share it for breakfast at the visiting faculty building. Anthony would have coffee and croissants with me over an extended morning, and we would start the day with reading cards, looking at planetary alignments, and talking about love. 'Who did it better?' I'd ask Anthony. 'Ben Jonson was better than Shakespeare in love,' Anthony would say, and then intone with a clear image in his mind: 'all those courtly masques…'

As befitting a genius who can recite by heart all of Shakespeare and all of Jonson, this Johnson was in love with none other than Helen of Troy, the beautiful shapeshifter. But it didn't work out. There's no irony here, given the man's love of masques/masks, so I wanted to know more. I didn't want to ask about communication that fails in the face of endless love — that also happened to him — as I didn't want to sound like a marriage counselor. For what do we actually mean when we put communication on a par with infinity? A ludicrous idea. But it was then that Anthony said to me, 'a cure for love is a greater love.' Then he sighed. 'So, the greater lover never happened after that?' I asked, to make sure I understood. He smiled: 'it never did.' It was my time to think about the idea of carrying inflamed torches and its consequences, but that wasn't it. It was more about carrying an image, rather than a beacon of light, to put it this way in the interest of optimism.

In common parlance, or indeed, in counseling settings, there's this prevalent notion that if you want to get over a great love, what you can do is either stop communicating or investing time in actually getting to know the other person better, so that their true colors, or some color that doesn't sit well with you, can emerge. Fair enough. On this, I like the simplicity of what poet Wendy Cope has to offer in her apt text, *Two Cures for Love*, a book that I happened to buy in Helsinki on another trip to Finland: '1. Don't see him. Don't phone or write a letter. 2. The easy way: get to know him better (Cope, 2008: 32).

As a visual person myself, I don't think that the first cure works, because all it takes is to conjure the image of the beloved before your eyes, and voilà, before you know it, you're already in conversation with this image. You don't actually need any of the suggested props for this conversation either, such as the physical phone or the writing of letters, as you can do it already in your head, and even be quite successful at it. The second cure holds more promise, for indeed, a person can come in all shades of gray, one more miserable than the other. I suppose that seeing too much greyness is enough to seal it, the decision to forget about the other and then leave it entirely at that, namely in the realm of self-induced amnesia.

It worked for Shakespeare's Romeo. When he went to make arrangements to be married to Juliet, the friar in charge was surprised to hear that the beloved was not Rosaline, the woman before Juliet, but rather the enemy. The friar admonished Romeo for his inconstancy, to which he replied along the lines that suggested that Juliet was now the greater love.

> I pray thee, chide not; she whom I love now
> Doth grace for grace and love for love allow;
> The other did not so. (2.3)

Romeo keeps it simple when he invokes his argument, for who can object to the woman who allows grace for grace and love for love? Romeo was saying it like it was: 'this is this.' But what happens when 'this is this' turns into something else? We already know what happened to Romeo and Juliet. They died. 'Coincidence happens,' Anthony offered and shared a series of synchronous events when he would stumble into Helen every time he would think of her harder than the usual daily habit. This, in spite of the fact that the woman had moved to another country. 'Was the love still there?' I asked, to which he said, 'oh yes,' but in a tone that left no room for the conjunctive query: 'and?' There was no 'and…' We looked at cards for this question instead: 'what magic binds eternal lovers?' Judgment, the Popess, and the Hanged Man were on the table.

'It's a spell,' I said to Anthony, 'it's the woman's written words that bind the man. But the condition is that there's a higher call that they both must hear. Their encounter is like the score of the Angel's song.' Now, I don't know anything about music, but Anthony does. So we talked about the sounds that are felt at the vibrational level creating a magnetic pull. Not all lovers can hear the blast from the infinite universe. The ones that do are in peril, for they feel the gravity of the whole thing weighing on them. The woman has a chance to survive this magical song, as she can translate it into words. Not so the man. He is at the mercy of the siren. So Juliet must tie a knot around Romeo's heel, in order to prevent him from sharing Achilles' fate. That's the bond. Eternal lovers are thus the poets of the world, living through rhyme and rhythm, analogy and metaphor, word and image.

Imagine a blast and a bond. Then Romeo who laments that he has no other choice than renunciation, because the situation doesn't help him. He can't be with Juliet because she is already tied to another. A classic. But what is not so classic is the blast and the bond. What of that? What spell can break the sound and the knot? Or are we here with their enforcement? A man wanted to know: 'I can't get closure. What can I do?' For once, I didn't get to see the Hanged Man on the table, as this card has a way of showing up all the time in questions about regret and situations that can't be helped. Instead I got these cards: the Sun, the Magician, and the Moon. A tall order for this Romeo caught between the two luminaries. Too much celestial power. Would changing the metaphors help? 'Not on my watch,' says the Moon, the very mistress of metaphors. What then? Can the Sun help? 'Yes, I can heat it for you,' it says. But unless this Magician is an idiot, he will know that heat is the last thing he needs in his business about closure. What he needs is to get cold on it. But can he? How does one break away from the eternal spell, the work of the infinite love itself? I said to Romeo: 'think about what you forgot. There is something you forgot. Go back to that, and when you remember it, think about your desire for closure. Will it still be there?'

Now, the implications of the inability to get closure is that when closure is withheld, the secret sets in. When love hurts because it doesn't seem to go anywhere — that is to say, to whatever is imagined as 'satisfaction' — lovers tend to think that the other has the power to give them closure. 'Give me closure,' Romeo can say to Juliet, exposing his powerlessness to her. When she says that she can't, because, lo and behold, she is equally unresolved in her love, the heart sinks. Intuitively lovers are correct in their assumption that closure must come from the other, but this is only possible if the other is free of her own thoughts about the relationship. What happens when this is not the case? A secret happens. Each can go about living their separate lives, but internally they will continue to enter the forbidden chamber, where the conversation with the lover still occurs in the innermost recesses of the mind. As long as the visions of the other are still conjured, and the other knows about it, the potentiality for closure is non-existent. So we're with a double bind here. I often read the cards for lovers whose hearts are still inflamed in spite of separation, and what I have observed is that the continuum of experiencing the other through imaging can occur regardless of how this other gets to live. Both men and women can say, 'I know what I know,' referring to their own emotional field, and in this knowing accommodate what invariably becomes the life of a secret unfolding in parallel with whatever else is experienced, other partners or geographies not shared with the 'lost' one.

The cards above speak of this very situation, as we go from the Sun, suggesting a time when all is clear, to the Moon, suggesting the opposite. Symbolically the Moon has been seen as the repository of secrets, shadows, and dreams. Topographically here, the Moon in the last position speaks of the impossibility to demolish the edifice of the imagination, not even when one has the Magician's skills. If the heart harbors a secret, snapping your fingers and saying *abracadabra* won't make it go away. So what's the solution? There isn't any. We're with what we call 'the inconsolable,' the heart's cold grief as a testimony to its love. If there's satisfaction in this love, then it is in the grieving lover's capacity to honor the image that maintains the other in the heart.

In my fortunetelling practice I have an eye for how this honor is transacted with, so that it becomes what we call 'manageable.' Why is this important? Well, think about it. Sometimes lovers come to me and say the following: 'I don't care about how the other thinks of me, or about how they see me, or about how they now live their lives. I know what I know. My love is beyond blame. But I would like to know whether I'm wasting my time. What do the cards say? Am I wasting my time, and how? The other still inspires me and I have no problems keeping the narratives apart: there's a public room and a secret room. We all live double lives.' Fair enough, especially since this is a common conundrum. But the question of wasting time *is* interesting, for we would all like to know how it manifests exactly, if it does at all.

Let's see what I mean here. A great love that turns into a love that's one-sided runs into the problem with anonymity. Think again about what Jean-Luc Marion says regarding the infinite conversation between lovers: 'the lover never finishes telling himself of the beloved, telling himself to the beloved, and telling the beloved to herself.' Think about the implications of this for the love that doesn't go anywhere. If this tripartite conversation can take place in a lover's head simultaneously, then the imaginary relation can be said to be symmetrical. If physical feedback is desired, then there's waste of time.

Now, obviously, when I read the cards for another who attempts to come to terms with how they can sink into the mirrors of their lovers, I don't sit and philozophize about it. What I do instead is look at how the cards trace their experience of the event of loving, either physically, when there's an encounter, or metaphysically, when an encounter is no longer possible. In this sense I engage with cartomancy from the point of view of cartography. Let me give a concrete example of what we may also term *cartographic cartomancy,* or the idea of tracing with the cards a lover's experience, memory, and projection of what is both lived in the sensual body and thought of in the imagination. I'll start first with a framing of what I mean.

When people come to the fortuneteller to ask a question, they do it out of how they experience an event, how they remember it, and how they project its consequences into the future. So every act of cartomantic transmission is bound to a process of tracing how this event is framed by the questioner's experience, remembrance, and projection of it. This framing is part of how a querent gives form to what they ultimately stage in their lives as a matter of purpose and course. The task of the fortuneteller is to know the difference between what is already staged and what lends itself to a useful tracing of what is staged so that the imaginary solution provided by the cards can actually beat the imagined reality of the situation.

If this sounds complicated, just think about it: as the experience of something is not the real thing, and neither is the memory or projection of it, what the fortuneteller transacts with as a matter of routine is permutations with fictions. Therefore, and counter-intuitively, what we actually do with the cards is not read them interpretatively, but rather, trace with them the form of what is framed already in the question. In other words, we operate with a superimposed map unto the cards, a map that traces our sense of what weighs more for a querent where their expectation is concerned.

In this sense our cartomancy starts with cartography, with mapping what a querent wants: more nuanced knowledge of their lived experience, or an actual understanding of how such knowledge can be processed so that it becomes an essential part of their lived wisdom. While the two are not mutually exclusive, you will note that there's a preference either for the one or the other, description or reflection. If a predictive element is desired, then it follows suit, with some predictions lending themselves to the 'what' of the situation and others inviting a reflection of 'how' it will all pan out.

To give an example of how this works in practice, imagine this scenario from a context regarding an argument between two lovers: 'we had a falling out, because he thinks I lied to him,' the woman says, implicitly both asking about how to cope with her indignation and, at the same time, staging her preparedness for defense, her eyes glaring: 'I didn't lie to him, but he thinks I did.' When the cards crack open this conundrum towards the imaginary solution, what they offer you is the possibility to trace this woman's experience, her memory of it that already contains distortion, and her projection of 'what will happen afterwards.' In this case here I got these cards: the Hanged Man, the Sun, and the Wheel of Fortune.

The cards enabled me to say this: 'you got hanged for your love because a third party was also caught in the wheel. Maybe you can keep the narratives apart – what the two of you have in common is your business, not the business of the third party involved – but if your lover can't keep these narratives apart, then there's no resolution, as that would require a re-configuration of the dynamics of the game.'

The imaginary solution that arises from this tracing can be formulated as a question to the querent: 'whose logic are you going to use? Yours? – two have nothing to do with the third – or his? – three is one too many in this relationship.' Whichever perspective you go with, the deeper implications of this also have to do with seeing the role of the Hanged Man in the first position. In some esoteric literature on the tarot this card is seen as a card of sacrifice and self-sacrifice. I'm not so keen on the latter idea, as it's unlikely that the Hanged Man hangs himself willingly by his foot. It's also more fascinating to consider that if he doesn't do it himself, then some other agent is involved. What is this external force or condition that the Hanged Man submits to? The universe, or some other more mundane manifestation? We want to know this, precisely because the Hanged Man situation relates to what we may perceive as 'wasted time.' Even when you decide that it's good to suspend your actions, you may still want to know for how long. But here, if indeed as suspected, the reading is about tracing a love triangle, then who is the sacrificing party and for what? Is the woman querent represented by the Hanged Man, or is the Hanged Man an actual representation of her lover who inadvertently accuses her of falling short of rising to his willingness to share his life with her under the Sun?

Whatever agency is embodied here, there is also this question: Are we with a sacrifice in the name of a principle or a promise? Is this sacrifice for defense, self-defense, or a higher, intangible purpose? Are we with the idea of continuity because a kinship is identified that exceeds all cultural codes? What of the third one caught in the wheel? How significant is this person? Finally, if this is not a case of self-undoing, then who, indeed, is sacrificing the Hanged Man, and more importantly, on whose altar is this sacrifice put? As we ask these questions, the wheel keeps turning… Consequently, just by reflecting on the above – and there can be more to think about – you get the sense that the only interpretation that cuts it is the one that actually attempts to trace all the lines that frame the plausible story. Some of these lines are distinct, while others are more subtle. The point is that in any act of observing what is happening in the cards, what you bring to this observation is your curious mind first, and only then your motivation.

Speaking of metaphors, if you want one here for your own cartographic cartomancy, you can imagine poring over your cards at a dark hour in one of those days when the only light is the moonlight, or the shimmer from your candle lit in your solitary cottage in the woods, tracing the obvious, hidden in the shadows of the souls that long for a magical touch. On such a day you don't interpret your cards as 'the first thing.' What you do instead is trace the whole arsenal of unarticulated emotions and map it unto the cards as a remembrance that activates your querent's awareness of impermanence. If there's a cold shiver around the heart, then your task as a fortuneteller is to warm it up and find the words of love that are not circumscribed by cliché. Then respond in kind.

Now, although this reading above was a reading about an argument that turned out to be precisely about tracing a love triangle, with the woman dividing her attention between two men, even when that was not put on the fortuneteller's table, you can extrapolate and see this same scenario in play in other types of relationships: at work, between bosses and colleagues, or at home, between spouses, parents and children. Whenever favoritism arises, or a re-shuffling of ranks especially when there's no clear ground for it, there's conflict: 'I used to work well with my boss, but he is now more invested in my co-worker whom I think is lazy,' or 'my eldest son developed envy towards my youngest, his brother, now projecting also the false notion that I favor the youngest over him.'

There's no end to how people stage their predicaments, even when they don't realize that when they present you with their situation, that is exactly what they do, frame it by remembering a particular emotion that sets the stage for this framing, and then project an expectation. Therefore the fortuneteller must have an eye for the way in which her cards move beneath this cartographic scene, and never lose her tracing line. That is to say, it pays off to read the cards with view to tracing the *form* that the querents give to their questions, as it is this form that discloses how a concern is framed and how a motivation is staged so that it yields a solution. In this sense, we could argue that knowing the heart of man is a question of method, if it is an aim beyond the intuitive, though how you get beneath the lines that merely give you a contour of what the other's fears are only comes with the practice of paying attention to what is articulated between the lines.

The hardest is to read for the eternal lovers who are not together, for how are you to tell them whether they waste their time or not, when they engage themselves in never finishing telling themselves of the beloved, telling themselves to the beloved, and telling the beloved to themselves? Some lovers are like the Israelites in exile. After 40 years of wandering in the desert, they don't give up. Rather, they re-enforce their commitment *in eternis*, declaring that regardless of the situation, they will henceforth be with their absent lover, if nothing other than for the sake of refining the art of waiting, still, for the potential that has already occurred. I don't want to say that my favorite time is when I get to read the cards for the endless story, that is to say, the story that can never finish precisely because it has never begun properly, but there's something of the highest romantic drama here that enables me to cut right to the core of just what knowing a man's heart is all about.

Most of the time, however, I read the cards for this question: 'what is she thinking of?' the implicit being a question about strategy, as in, 'what will she do next?' the implicit again being a question of whether Juliet is thinking of Romeo, essentially, for if she does, then the game is still on, and *that* is what lovers want to know: 'can I still have her, or am I wasting my time?'

– the implicit yet again being a question about desire, namely the desire to continue to have access to controlling the act of giving or withholding closure. The beauty about lovers is that, ultimately, they would risk their own lives for this, as it's no different than driving a Formula One car, when you work with the approximation of speed and distance in relation to both what the car can do and what you can do in it, or when you listen to a Bach fugue and are ready to swear that although you can hear the *contrapunctum*, you declare that it doesn't exist, thus defeating entirely its intended purpose.

When Sir Thomas Urquhart (1611-60) translated the works of François Rabelais (1490-1551), he coined a new concept that placed the counterpoint – which is strictly speaking the opposite of the point – in direct analogy to the man and woman's sexual organs. What does Juliet want? Less sermonizing and pointing of the finger and more seizing of her openness towards the infinite world. The cure for love must be *en garde*.

Romeo wants to drive

Juliet likes fast cars. She doesn't drive the most expensive one, even though a rich Capulet. She has a red Mini Cooper S Coupé as it matches her white gloves.

Romeo wants to drive with her to the end of the world. He is not sure he can get in the car, what with his size, but he is intent on watching Juliet rally. His eyes are hungry for her hands. As he also has a penchant for gloves, his excitement is perfect.

Would she touch his knee while shifting the gears? But Juliet is not into seductive acts. Not when she is driving. When Juliet gets behind the wheel, she is under necrocratic rule. Dead Ayrton Senna checks her wheels and then takes a seat in the rear window. They call this a spirit consortium.

Romeo is apprehensive of this bond, but oh, the engine. A re-empowerment of his imagination. He can almost observe what is invisible to him.

Juliet's armor

'THE WALL MOVED.' 'No, it didn't.' 'Yes, it did, a few millimeters, and it was in my way. That's why I crashed.' This is Ayrton Senna talking, explaining why he couldn't finish a car race in Dallas when he had all the odds with him. As reported by race engineer, Pat Symonds, someone had hit the far end of the concrete block resulting in the track swiveling, so that the leading edge of the block was standing out by a few millimeters. That was enough to make the difference. How could Senna see that? Sense that?

I like this story so much about Ayrton Senna, the legendary Brazilian Formula One driver and God of precision, because it makes me understand why, when he died in 1994, the Japanese cried the hardest. This in spite of the fact that Senna at that point was no longer associated with the Japanese, racing for Honda. Although no one has ever wondered about it, I like to think of a reason. As the Japanese are invested in the concept of *kokoro*, or the things done with the heart from a standpoint of no compromise, of a death resolve, I like to see how this *kokoro* crosses national borders, making everyone a samurai, that is to say, if they are able to display it. Senna could. He was just like the most famous swordsman Miyamoto Musashi, who understood timing and precision in the context of death. You draw the sword too early, you're dead. Too late, you're also dead. You break too early, you're dead. You lose the competition. You break too late, you're also dead. You lose your life. There's a lot of mastery that goes into knowing the difference. The masters who possess such knowledge also raise this difference to the status of art. This means that they get inscribed into my book of conjurations. I call on their dead souls and ask them to teach me how I can risk being blown off course, yet without losing it.

As it happens, I'm not into cars and Formula One drivers, except for the fact that I got a taste for it when, in the early '80s, I watched the French film *Un Homme et une Femme* by Claude Leloush (1966), featuring the love story between a car racer who lost his wife to suicide and a widow who lost her husband to an accident. But as I drive through town and the quiet Danish landscape, I have Senna on my mind. When I get behind the wheel I call on him, as I'm always curious to know how he'd compete when there's no competition around, for I'm sure he'd find something to race against.

I pay for this privilege: I smoke a pipe and eat Brazilian chocolate. I dedicate the hedonism to Senna. I also read the cards. As Senna was an inveterate Catholic who regularly performed bibliomantic seances by reading verses from the Bible at random that he would then take as the oracular voice of the divine guiding him through the day, I think that he would approve of the Devil's work here, the name cartomancy happens to go by. To keep it with the martial arts *kokoro*, I offer Senna my Mars pipe, a sweeter chocolate than I personally prefer, and the Carolus Zoya Marseille Tarot in the form of a haiku. Three cards fall on the table: Justice, the Devil, and Force.

As this reading is a way to thank him for all he did, and also for accompanying me on my own car trips, giving me instruction even as I have to suffer through plodding along at the lowest speed behind some geriatric — myself joining that club soon enough — I see these cards as a representation of what he was like: a man of justice and a daredevil of great caliber. In the form of a haiku, however, here's what I see:

When the time is right
The hot Devil rides once more
Helmet of ardor

I like Senna because he operated with simple truths. He knew what his own justice was. His triumvirate was made up of determination, dedication, and competence. Justice here is the woman of method. Competence stems from methodical awareness and self-reflection. Force has the helmet of infinity on, overcoming all obstacles. The Devil says, 'if you want it badly enough, then resolve to go for it. Go all in and give it your all without compromise.'

I can't think of better cards for Senna. The Chariot in the tarot, the car, didn't present itself on my table, as one might have expected. But then I'm not surprised, as he was done with that. Senna wasn't done with racing, but he was done with the car. What we got here instead is the exactitude of 'neither too much, nor too little, but precisely as much as it's necessary.' There's no space for the millimeters that push our walls off track and chance. We can't afford to crash because of it.

CAN I GO ALL IN?

This is a question I often get from Romeo and Juliet. Yes, times have changed since Shakespeare. Although love remains a gamble, fools don't always rush in. Nowadays fools are cautious, as they are not under dictations from the higher virtues. Courage has been replaced by cautiousness. Heroism has been replaced by a heralding voice: 'I am successful. Look at me now.' Image overrules passion. Sometimes I want to blurt at the anguished Romeo: 'why don't you just do it, go all in, fall head over heels? What do you need the cards for? What do you expect them to say? Give you permission, because giving permission is in vogue?' I don't say any such things, though, as I like to take Romeo's money for my oracular service. Besides, on occasion, and more often than not, actually, Romeo is advised to show restraint. The trio formed by the Charioteer, the Tower, and Death on my table is not a good omen.

I arm myself against the faltering emotions, and then say, 'don't do it, man. You'll lose your life.' But Romeo is in love. Will he listen? Some do. Most don't. They come to me after their seven years of itches and report on how Juliet is now taking them to court. She wants half the house *and* the sports car. I mean, can you believe having to relinquish your Lamborghini? Even *I* would have a hard time with that, and I'm not that much into cars. What I see in the cards Romeo can also see. Then I bank on what Shakespeare said: 'Young men's love then lies not truly in their hearts but in their eyes' (2.3). See, that's exactly what I'm talking about, using your eyes...

November

Romeo committed harakiri leaving Juliet in a state of haze. This was after the time when she had an epiphany one gloom day in November. She canceled that beginning of her winter, and this made Romeo decide that all was lost. He did the right Japanese thing.

But Juliet is a magician. It doesn't matter to her whether Romeo is dead or alive, as she specializes in corpses. She can reanimate them with two snapping fingers. Will she do it again? For what purpose?

'The dead always speak the truth,' the sages say, so hearing the truth is a good reason to bring back the dead. But Juliet vacillates. She has the bad habit of knowing many truths. What can the dead lover tell her that she doesn't know already?

Romeo is moving in his grave. Accidentally Juliet touches his bones. 'O Romeo, Romeo! wherefore art thou a martial artist?'

Juliet is 53

I AM WAITING FOR A VERDICT. 'When it all started, did you think about something very intensely, being focused on it?' the doctor specializing in chronic illnesses wants to know. He figured that he was facing an affliction that befalls intellectuals. 'Yeah,' I say, 'like everyday,' confirming the stereotype. He nods, yet he thinks there's more. He wants me to be more specific. But I don't volunteer more information. I'm the discrete type. Besides, this is not the kind of information that he absolutely needs to get. Then he asks me if I smoke. 'Not really,' I say, telling him the truth. 'I only smoke a ritual pipe.' 'A ritual pipe?' he asks with his eyebrows raised. 'That's right,' I say, and leave it up to him to conjure an image of just what that means. 'Damn,' he says. 'I can't tell you to start smoking, as the other docs would be after me, but you know, this is the only disease that gets better with some smoke in it.' Now it's my time to nod, and pledge to increase my pleasure. I'm thinking about the indigenous people who are on to something when they do it for peace.

Smoke, that is. I'm sure there are other reasons too that they don't feel obliged to share with us, Westerners, as yet. While the good doc is explaining what the deal is, my head is already filled with Latakia, Périque, Virginia, Burley and Black Cavendish. Although I smoke aromatic tobaccos, I'm what you'd call an 'Oriental girl' through and through. Some of this stuff can raise the dead, and I like to see that when it happens.

An aging woman invested in reading signs only gets better at it the more she loses her body. She may need reading glasses too, but the older she gets the sharper her vision. Throw into it a good tobacco blend, and you're in for precision. In the right mood, the fortuneteller can get to the heart of man in a split second. Smoke beats horse power. This is because some smoke enforces non-separation. We're not with the fortuneteller reading the cards for the young woman in love who reminds her of herself. No. She reads for herself. She is Juliet. At 53. The 16 year old is now part of a blend, releasing its flavor in the company of other mature manifestations.

I don't want to say that I'm astonished, but it never ceases to amaze me when I encounter an old Juliet who forgets about her age, and in the course of this forgetfulness, she discloses her true heart. *Now* she is in love and the time stands still. It's as if no other time has ever existed. Nothing entertains me more than the right kind of transgression. Imagine to disclose your true heart at the age of 53. It doesn't happen. I'm 53 and I disclose nothing. You might call me the tragic type. I can read the cards to precision and pierce strongly into another's heart, but disclose my own heart? I'm not even sure that the Romeo who sits in the middle of the fire, my volcano, can make me do it. Not publicly, anyway. So I read the cards for the other people's hearts. Let's see what I mean. Three fall on the table: the Hanged Man, the Emperor, and the Devil.

The perceptive woman in love will note the following: 'I'm not in the picture at all. There isn't a single card here that represents me.' 'No,' I say, 'not directly,' and then point to the phrasing of her question: 'Knock, knock. Are you still there?' This is actually her query, as she wants to know if the lover she lost touch with is still there. To be more specific, 'there' here refers to the woman's sense of time standing still. So what she wants to know is if Romeo is still there, in her frozen time, in spite of his sudden death from unnatural causes. According to Juliet's story, Romeo declared his heart dead where she was concerned. But as this Juliet is not 16 anymore, she has her doubts. What if Romeo is full of shit? It happens all the time that people say one thing and mean another.

This situation is called mis- and missed communication. Most relationship questions that I get from people spring out of a failure to communicate, the most common expectation being that communication needs to exist, otherwise, no relationship. I'd say this is a fallacy. Some relationships work just fine without the clichés regarding 'clear communication,' 'transparency,' and 'honest talk.' When I hear lovers presenting me with these very expectations, namely that the communication be clear, transparent, and honest, what I also hear is a passive-aggressive threat, a demand. Not that anything is wrong with the clear, the transparent, and the honest, but when they are in demand with the indignant, something else is going on.

Depending on what the cards show, I often entice people to simply shut up and relax. While words can fix a lot of miscommunication problems, words are also notorious for ruining just about everything. How to tell the difference? That's the art. Cards or no cards, I have a preference for the communication that's simply sublime, the type that's not based on a set of business-sounding agendas. When I hear lovers say to one another, 'we need to talk,' I have the urge to run, as I see a river of muddy waters running through this demand, often deeply steeped in the desire to control the other, to take the upper hand. 'Oh, for fuck's sake, just shut up,' I say to the couples I read the cards for, and point to strategies of seduction instead. Might there be something in between the boringly constructed 'clear' and 'transparent' situation? I often think about how our relationships would change if we replaced the word 'communication' with the word 'seduction.' I could write a whole book about just that, and maybe I will, since that's my trade...

Meanwhile, with these reflections in mind, let's get back to Juliet's cards and listen to how I went about it, answering the woman's question about whether or not her lover was still there, hearing her. I said: 'yes, this Romeo is going nowhere. Declaring his heart dead didn't work. He's still hanging in there, feeling as well the seductive pull. He may want to take stock of what's binding him, but getting out of it is not an option. Not with the Devil handling the ropes.'

'But he never says anything,' the woman exclaimed, and I went, 'oh, just shut up. What makes you think that communicating is only subject to words? There's a reason why you're not in the picture here, and that's because you don't make an effort to pay attention to something other than words.'

I have to admit that I like to shame people when the occasion for it is just right. Some simply don't get it, ending up ruining a perfectly good relationship because they serve clichés about communication to the other they're in love with. Bad idea, for great love is never about clichés. It's about sensing in the other what you can never see, which is another way of saying that you sense their obviousness. Just as people don't disclose their true hearts, whether they are 16 or 53, they don't disclose their obviousness either, often for fear of being ridiculed. The task of the lover is to go past this fear, and point to the concreteness of the other's direct experience in relation to the loved one. How does it manifest?

Even Mercutio, Romeo's friend in Shakespeare's play, could intuit what was obvious, in the sense also of having a premonition when he referred to Romeo's death from love, before the other, physical death occurred. 'Alas poor Romeo! he is already dead; stabbed with a white wench's black eye; shot through the ear with a love-song' (2.4). Mercutio here makes a very specific transmission about the nature of love, by using vivid language to conjure the obvious, namely that love is violent and that it has consequences. Although it didn't go so well with Shakespeare's Romeo and Juliet, at least they died honorably. Together. Their true feelings demonstrated. These days people crash and burn without honor. Why? Because they communicate without their senses. Three cards falling on the table can be revealing of many things that are missing, rather than merely showing who is in the picture and competing for what attention.

In our example above, while the woman pointed to the obvious, 'I'm not in the picture,' she forgot her question, which was all about him: was he true to his heart when he killed it, or when he declared that his heart was now dead? Logically speaking, how can you honor a dead heart from the heart? Something is wrong with the correlation here. So when Juliet simply wanted to know if Romeo was 'full of shit,' as she literally put it, what she did in the moment she posed her question was to actually sense the other's obviousness in the face of the impossibility to follow up on the aberrant decision. The cards corroborated her intuition, suggesting in fact the presence of an obsession with ties: the Hanged Man is tied, and so are the two imps that the Devil controls, the lower order 'Romeo and Juliet' who don't act in accordance with their true will.

In this case here, it may well have been that Romeo's hand was guided towards *sepukku*, but he missed, as the gut is not the heart. The obvious, then, is to assume that as long as the heart is still beating, it can be revived by the proper touch, for a woman who knows the heart of a man, can also touch it if she chooses to, in that special way that's called the gift of poetry. What poetry does for a relationship is carry the mark of true commonality shared by lovers. As they mirror the images of self and the world into the other, they recognize the mood they're in, when they script the book they're living, including its rhyming verses and analogies. What we find in the metaphor of Romeo and Juliet touching one another with their gaze is their shared image of one another that is *exactly* the same.

The beauty of this exact image is that it makes the lovers stop from questioning one another: 'what do you want from me?' as the answer to this query is already a given. Exchanging what is already a given must be the highest aim, as it bypasses what is otherwise only perceived as the illusion of commonality. As having things in common does not equal carrying the same god, or sharing the same image that makes up a validated cosmology, what our modern Romeo and Juliet must seek is how to perfect the look in their eyes that touches the other in exactly the way in which the other imagines to be touched. That's the art, to recognize the image of the other as it is. This, then, sparks a sense of wonder: 'you are *exactly* like me.'

After this session and sermon my Juliet said, 'I need a cigarette, and I don't even smoke.' I opened my tobacco cabinet, including all the secret drawers, and together we plotted to bring Romeo back from the dead.

Conquest of the useless

Flashback, Werner Herzog style. Juliet made wedding preparations. She was going to marry Romeo at the Crystal Cathedral in the Arctic. They would cruise up to the place through the icebergs. She booked a whole goddamn boat for it. But he had to come first. He didn't. He sent her a cryptic note instead, blabbering something about Rosaline and a cathedral in Italy. Juliet said, 'fine.' She cursed him with descent into the crypt, while praising her own good sense. The cathedral she picked had no such gloomy place, so no mad lover could ever send her to it in case things would take a cold turn. She made a bonfire in the middle of the snow field and burnt all the papers intended for the consecration of the vows. Juliet always handled bureaucratic matters with utmost reverence. She recited the law of consummation by flames and then sang **Dies Irae**. Romeo's 'yes' had no spark in it, his nerve lost to frankincense and a faint smell of calandre.

The heart of man

THERE IS THIS PREJUDICE among diviners that if Romeo and Juliet split and they stay that way for a number of years, they never get back together again. This prejudice is almost as bad as the assumption that men and women repeat patterns, such as falling in love with the same type that broke their hearts, or what's worse, falling in love with the so-called 'unavailable' lovers. Before I even put any cards on the table, I often say this: 'you fall for the one you fall for. How can this falling have anything to do with availability? If the lover is available or not is beside the point. If your feelings are reciprocated, then this falling is a great gift. So what pattern are we talking about here?'

This idea with repeating patterns is not something I can comprehend, as love doesn't work that way, with thinking and calculating and assessing how sticky the situation is or not. That's nonsense. People set themselves up for moral evaluations and considerations of what is right or wrong in terms of what is culturally sanctioned. You're a bad person if you fuck a woman who is 'unavailable.' But if she responds to you and reciprocates your feelings, is this not love, the sublime that's pierced by the desire to have the other? What has morality got to do with the sublime? Nothing. What has availability got to do with the infinite love that you have to give? Nothing. Love doesn't operate with patterns that you repeat. It's not about the past and who else you fell for when the lightning struck. It's not about how terribly that went, or about how hard you're now trying to avoid repeating the past. Love is about the recognition that the other is exactly like you. The manners of doing things may be different and the characters may be different, but on the essential level, the level that gets the head leveled, there's a perfect mirror. What goes into love that's not conditioned by 'patterns' is a certain kind of relentlessness that makes the dream of it a reality.

'But it's useless,' sometimes Romeo laments, when he has to justify his fatal mistakes. 'I picked the second best, because the first best was not available.' This is a statement that's even more tragic than what Shakespeare had in mind when he wrote his immortal play. What is useless? Isn't love about being relentless, about conquests, the most sublime of them being the conquest of the useless? It's a problem when lovers lack the power of the imagination, when they can't visualize an outcome. A lover lacking magical skills is a lover that lacks virility. *That* is useless.

In his beautiful book written as a sustained reflection on how you get a 320-ton boat over a mountain so that your film featuring the deranged, yet sublime actor Klaus Kinski can happen, Werner Herzog takes stock of what it means to think in terms of magical solutions. So many things went wrong with the filming of *Fitzcarraldo* (1982), obstructing Herzog's love and relentlessness in pursuing his dream, that he had an idea. What if he kept a journal in which he would imagine the worst possible that could happen as a means of canceling the very possibility of more disaster to occur? Once taken place in the imagination, there would be no reason any more for the unexpected to hit.

I haven't seen anybody else referring to Herzog's practice as falling in the category of what we might call talismanic writing, but as far as I'm concerned, what Herzog gave us in his *Conquest of the Useless* is precisely a grimoire, a recipe for averting evil and its deployment in the passions of the heart. The work was written in minuscule handwriting to the point of the indecipherable, mirroring precisely the idea of dreams and their pursuit. It was only after some 25 years since its inception that this writing found its way to the larger public, and this, only at the behest of Herzog's wife, who insisted: 'if you don't publish it yourself, some idiot editor will get his hands on the manuscript after your death, and will misrepresent it.' This was not an option. Herzog could not let anyone tamper with the 'ecstatic truth' that he was after. The way of the ecstatic truth is the way of the relentless love that 'writes' its own form. Love in its highest manifestation is about form. Love's content would be the identification of useless ideas such as patterns, significations, the meaning of vows, future prospects that include calculating the presence of children and a good job in order for the notion that 'they then lived happily ever after' to be credible. But who are we kidding?

I once read the cards for a woman who wanted to make a choice. Give in to her flirtatious, yet unavailable colleague at work in the valley, or try her hand at love with another man she knew who lived on top of a mountain. 'I might get an opening towards love with the man in the wilderness,' she said. I noticed the way in which she phrased her predicament. It was filled with assumptions and permeated by the underlying presupposition that the fling with the colleague would be useless compared to the other potential. 'Am I repeating a pattern here, by falling for unavailable men?' she also quickly added, committing the fallacy of thinking that the potential for love can only find the ones who are available. What a nasty idea.

I put the cards down for each of the situations, the one in which she stayed in the valley and the other in which she would go to the mountain. The two pictures were quite telling in their contrast. For the flirting Romeo, Juliet got these cards: the Magician, the Fool, and the Empress.

I offered the following insight: 'if you stay in the valley, you'll develop a relationship with the co-worker who flirts with you. After putting on quite the seductive, dazzling act, the fool rushes in, going for you.'

In contrast to these cards, we looked at the other set representing the possibility to move to the mountain. For this one Juliet got Temperance, the Star, and the Popess.

These cards were also very clear. I offered the following reflection: 'you'll go to a place of temperate passion. You'll have peace there, quite literally getting high on the crisp air that will transport you to another level that's not tangible. Maybe too much peace. If love is on the agenda, I'm afraid that the cards say that it won't happen. To be sure, you'll be ready to strip naked for this man, but he won't be interested. So you'll end up taking the position of the nun, solitary, single woman, surrounded by books.'

Which option was better here for this woman? A good question, as it came down to what the woman wanted. While neither of the situations suggested a true Romeo and Juliet romance, the first scenario had more potential, even if only sex was in the picture to begin with. At least the woman could get to feel like an Empress, while the flirt went on. I enticed her to go for this option, if feeling loved was what she wanted. The cards showed that the other would give her due attention.

In the second option I saw her as the one who was willing to serve and also embody celestially high ideals and altruism, but would this get her satisfaction, make her feel like a woman in love? Hardly, as it was not likely that this sentiment would be reciprocated.

I frankly told the woman to stop thinking about the other's availability. If he was already flirting with her, then obviously he was available for something. Sometimes this something is enough. It's a beginning. 'Conquer the useless,' I said, 'it takes time to build a cathedral. Some you can build yourself in your imagination. You can let it sing a song of ice instead of fire for you. It will be enough to quench your thirst. It is for this reason that such a cathedral will be more durable.'

SPELLS

Writing can instantiate a state of crisis. It can also maintain a crisis, or use a state of crisis to perform a miracle. The fountain pen is the magic wand. Now only to know how to give form to words. It's almost the same with the reading of cards. The function of words is to spell things out. Their very form is that of a spell itself, supporting the general idea that 'if you can name it, it exists.' Throw into it the use of breath, voice to say it out loud, and a hand whose touch is conscious, and you're in for the ecstatic truth.

On occasion I get requests from lovers with broken hearts to create a sigil, a special kind of writing with ink on parchment or rare Japanese paper, that would enhance the possibility for a reconciliation. 'Impossible, no matter how great the hope, Romeo doesn't just return to Juliet,' some other diviners and magical practitioners say, because of statistics. But what is the reality of it? I often ask the anguished lovers to tell me about the state of their deaths: 'just how dead is the heart?' The one hoping still has a pulsating one. What about the other? I'm always interested to know what goes behind the heart of man, that is to say, what is behind what is declared. 'He said his heart is dead where I am concerned,' Juliet often says, and I get excited. 'Good,' I say. 'This is excellent.' For in my experience with words, what I've come to learn is that if you have to tell people that you are, you aren't. If you have to tell people that your heart is dead where another is concerned, then it isn't.

I take this assumption as my starting point for my magical operations. As I also read Juliet's heart, the heart that also knows that what it is being served is not true, I probe the territory of what it takes for a transaction to occur. 'What are you willing to give up for it?' I ask Juliet, referring to her payment in exchange for Romeo's heart. If she says, 'my own sanity,' then we're in business. The portal towards accessing the ecstatic truth is open. Without this truth, there's no magic.

Grimoire magic relies on the crafting of spells through the vehicle of magic words in order to achieve a specific outcome. The words that go into it may not follow the conventions of rational thinking, rules of grammar, and recognizable vocabulary. To this day, we still wonder what a magic word such as *abracadabra* means. The magic that goes into it consists of a tight formalism that operates with design, from typography and the shape of the letters to sound. Symmetry, rhyme, and rhythm overrule symbolic signification. In order for the word *abracadabra* to work, raise the dead or perform some other such impossible feat, it needs to hinge on a performative gesture. Whether the word means anything at all is beside the point compared to this gesture, as the word's signification, or semantic content, is secondary to the performative aim.

Take what a film director does when he declares his intent behind the camera: 'roll' and 'cut' are not just commands that signal the action. Rather, they are also performative locutions geared towards obtaining an effect. In this sense the commands are magical, as they perform what they do. The same applies to how Romeo and Juliet perform the consecration of their vows. When they say 'I do' in the cathedral, they perform their intent to be bound until 'death do us part.' Where the words as such are concerned, both lovers and film directors might as well say *abracadabra,* since this magic word would perform the intended symbolic action exactly in the same way as the words that we recognize as part of the vocabulary that's appropriate for each specific setting. Where a marriage ritual is concerned, it's amusing to think that there's no difference between what the church does and what some other invested authority does, as the script for 'I do' follows the form of the grimoire, the book of magic spells and spirit conjurations. If words are to achieve a magical aim, they must be invested with wings; they must be inspirited. That this is a primary condition is given in thinking of the inverse of the situation. I bet that even the lovers who are ignorant of the way ritual works would be worried, if, for whatever reason, they would perceive their 'I do' as lacking in strength, being devoid of just the necessary spirit that goes into uttering the words in a way that's not faltering. I have witnessed wedding ceremonies when I felt that one of the lovers would have desired to say 'cut, let's say it again with the proper sound coming out of it.' But they never go for a second take, jinxing their chance to get it right.

In *Conquest of the Useless* there's a passage in which Herzog recounts an incident about Kinski's legendary rage, manifest in beating the crap out of his Vietnamese wife at the time of shooting *Fitzcarraldo*. Kinski would get her up the wall, leaving her senseless, with blood splattered all over the place, blood that would be discretely washed away in the early morning hours, so the other guests at the hotel in Machu Pichu they were staying at would be spared the sight. Herzog says that it took him years to even talk about this, lamenting perhaps his inability to say, 'cut, enough of this already.' But why couldn't he say the magic words? Well, it's simple. It wasn't his table. This wasn't his story to tell. It was not his place to interfere.

As ironic as it sounds, what we find in this inability to intervene was his placing agency with Juliet. It was her call to say, 'cut.' Why didn't she? Some Indian chiefs Herzog worked with offered to kill Kinski. They also had enough of the man's erratic behavior. Herzog declined. A wise man. Imagine what would have happened. Juliet didn't want her Romeo killed. If that had happened, would she have found a magical way to revive his heart? Would she have brought him back from the dead? She was in love with the man, after all, which is the reason why she allowed him his transgressions. The ethically oriented ones would have a different view of the situation, perhaps being more ready to 'save' the woman. But would that have changed her heart? How?

It is awfully important to know your place. People acting on behalf of a cause are often blind to this wisdom. They pass judgment on another's heart without actually knowing the heart. This is bad. You almost want to say to the saviors: 'save yourselves instead' — say it in a magical tone that's permeated with the symbolic intentional action that recognizes the sovereignty of the other, however miserable a state they may find themselves in. It's up to Juliet herself to issue her curse or the conjuration that would render her uncut from the Romeo she loves. And then if she so fancies, bring him back from hell, provided that he turns in his grave, saying in a magical tone too: 'I made a mistake.' Once this ground is laid, then the healing touch can be applied to the still throbbing heart.

Some may say that this is a naive way of romaticizing a love. But is this really so? What logic would account for this assumption? I'm looking for it and can't find it. In Shakespeare's play we don't find such ambiguities. Romeo is convinced that Juliet is done for, and instead of taking a moment to think about it, he decides to take his own life. Shakespeare's Romeo was no real magician. Had he been one, he would have said, 'nothing is final until I say so.' Juliet already had her death initiation. Why couldn't he wait to see what would happen, had he said those words? He saw her on the catafalque and he lost his nerve. But every tradition has its way of attending to the dead through a wake. You give yourself time before you attend to the burial of the body. You sing a song and go through a few memories. Why didn't Romeo do that? Had he done it, he would have lived to see Juliet rise up again. Instead, his kiss of her dead body was not inspirited enough. It lacked conviction. That's the real tragedy. Shakespeare's Romeo was full of presumptions, full of claiming Juliet as his own. If he lost his life like an idiot, it's because he was afflicted by the demon called possessiveness. He was the bereaved lover of the other who was never his. When Juliet woke up, she might have been merciful. She might have offered him her magic hand, or the words of magical incantations placing her in the infinite potential. But she also lost her nerve, giving in to the illusion that if she couldn't be his, she wouldn't be anyone else's.

The point about infinite love is that it remains incomprehensible to the human mind. Call it a magical mystery. We find this mystery at the heart of all serious relationships, as it is not informed by the desire to know the other, let alone possess them. Thus, we're here with this mystery's potential to reveal itself unto us as a chance to experience the ineffable beyond measure. We cannot betray the game of the ineffable. It is the role of infinity to hide the disappearing numbers — 'I will love you, but for how long?' — and yet it is our role to guess their function. We can thus sentence ourselves to counting, if and only if we cannot do any better.

Thinking with Demons

Romeo grabs Juliet by her waist and then presses his head against her bosom. Time stands still. Although she likes to count, she knows that they're now in the uncountable. The memory of this moment will subsume all the other memories for eternity.

When Romeo pushes her away again, she knows that he is trying to discredit evil. The evil of passion. But Juliet knows Romeo's heart, because he insists on showing it to her in spite of his better judgment. On his bedside table there's a big black book: **Thinking with Demons**.

If Juliet was not well versed in reading signs, she would ask the question: why is Romeo reading such books? But she doesn't ask the question. She licks her index finger instead, and touches Romeo's forehead. Now they're even.

Return to *passion*

THEY ARE EMBEDDED IN LANGUAGE: hope, fear and desire. It is more often the case that while men decide on a course of action, women ask: 'could we do this?' The use of 'we' here also discloses anxiety, for most of the time, if you asked women about it, what they would rather say is this: 'could *I* do this?' yet secretly, of course, wishing to dispense altogether with the modal imposition, and banish it from their vocabulary; no more could, would, and should.

In my own life and time as a woman, I can't even recall hearing men asking their consorts: 'could we do this?' in reference to whatever trivial or serious matter. In contrast, I've witnessed many times the inverse of the situation. Now, culturally speaking, there's a reason for this. It's called having control over the bank account. But it seems that no matter how emancipated women are these days and how much more they can earn compared to their partners, when it comes to the acquisition of a house, a car, or a holiday, women go, 'could we do this?' The slightest deviation from this ingrained cultural convention can lead to conflict, its culmination often being a manifestation of a range of reactions and responses, from complete denial of the woman's wish to gaslighting, as in 'no, we can't do this' to 'you're nothing without me.' The woman who can think for herself might expect an argument if the first scenario is the case, but she would be waiting in vain for that which would have no correlation to what was initially put on the table – if the second scenario is being served – as it's hard to see how we can go from the statement 'no, we can't get this house' to 'you're nothing without me.'

I like it that Shakespeare's Juliet named her terms when it comes to articulating her desire: 'if you're serious about your love,' she said to Romeo, 'come back here with the marriage papers, and I'll give myself to you.' Of course, given their fate, it's hard to speculate to what extent Juliet might have been able to continue to use her authoritative voice whenever she wanted something, but chances are that she would also have run into a few objections made, not in the name of reason, but rather for the sake of maintaining the patriarchal order. Passion or no passion, some things don't just change. Or, let us ask for our entertainment: can passion overrule conditioning?

I read the cards for conflicts all the time, and I'm always interested in noticing where there is a swerve from the language of passion to the language of constraint. I've already made the point that if we observe Shakespeare's play carefully, we note that the playwright infuses Juliet's language with the limitless, while letting Romeo speak in the idiom of limits. Romeo is simply more prone to flinging clichés at Juliet, while it's clear that she is on an altogether other level. So the tension here is really between limits and the limitless. This means that while the man can say yes or no, thus limiting himself and the other to a concrete plane of action, if the woman is in the limitless, she can go beyond the expression of dualistic thought.

I see this at work in all sorts of questions from people having relationship problems. What interests me always is to figure out who is speaking what language, for indeed, the limit and the limitless can be embodied by both genders, with some men being very capable of abstract thought, and some women preferring the pragmatic side of things. Let me give an example. Once a woman had a particular desire for a car. Being more advanced in her language, she asked her partner: 'could *I* have it?' instead of the more inclusive, 'could *we* have it?' The man took a look at her choice and decided that the car was inappropriate for her age. So she posed this question to the cards: 'just what car is an appropriate car for a woman?'

I liked this question very much, especially since the cards also had something interesting to say. For this question she got the Queen of Coins, the Ace of Batons, and the Emperor. Before I even got to say anything, the woman asked rhetorically, 'so, the only car that's appropriate for a woman, even when she can pay for it herself, is the one that her partner must endorse?' Her finger was pointing to the phallic looking Ace of Batons, whose strong presence here was hard to miss. Indeed, the woman's question was a good question, though we might think that what the cards have to say here may also be related to the idea that an appropriate car for a queen is the type that can accommodate enthusiastically her partner. And yet her question was, 'could *I* have it?' She didn't say, 'could *we* have it?' There's nothing like precision in language.

What the cards showed here is exactly a relationship of dependency, one that is very much maintained by societal norms. Juliet may wish to drive in the car of her preference, but there are still factors to consider when it comes to the notion of appropriateness. And yet, what do we do when this notion runs counter to the heart's desire? Does the heart care much about image and respectability? Where this particular subject is concerned, I have to admit that I have as yet to see a man who will refuse his heart's desire, no matter how old he is. He will go for the car of his dreams, if he can afford it, irrespective of the potential critique of inappropriateness that he may also be subject to. We do hear a lot about how men 'compensate' for their lack of virility with a red Ferrari. We may all laugh at Romeo, but meanwhile, the fun is with him. Whatever his motivation, he is driving the fast, red devil. What of Juliet?

AN OLD LOVE AFFAIR

My mother was 40 when my father died. He was younger. They had 14 years together as a married Romeo and Juliet. I'm not sure what kind of a relationship they had, but this I know: he recognized her as a genius. This means that he trusted her to make the right decisions, so she was fortunate enough to not have a problem with her voice. Her voice was strong and unwavering. When she decided, 'we do it like this,' he just said 'fine.' They were both skilled at calculating, given that one was a mathematician and the other a logician. Mother liked syllogisms. Father liked symmetries. When he died mother got all the numbers, deciding everything without asking for permissions. Sometimes she thought *this* was genius. Other times she needed a variation on the imaginary solutions, before they became a reality. That's when she would divine for it. She used the Bible as a bibliomantic tool and read coffee beans. But most of all she liked the clarity of a well-wrought phrase, when found at random and by chance, yet when also called for.

When she was 45 she decided to get a car. She had seen an add in a newspaper that someone had a Fiat 500 for sale at a price that sounded good. Although mother knew nothing about cars and didn't have a driver's license, something told her that she must go see it. She brought a mechanic along. He gave her the green light. Then she thought some more about it and finally decided: 'that's it, I'll do it. I've no idea how I'll pay for it, but I'll do it.' She wanted me to accompany her for the final transaction. This was exciting, as I liked visiting old Jewish doctors who lived in *Jugendstil* houses in communist

Romania, who drove a Fiat 500. A perfect car for us, as the three women in my family were what you'd call petite. I could see that not only could we get in the car, but we could also make some space for a Romeo, if we found one.

'Hello, hello,' the old doctor said, and mother replied, 'hello, I'm back.' 'So, you're ready for the car?' he asked her, and she said, 'yes, I have everything you need with me.' 'Wonderful,' he said, while glancing at me, as if waiting to hear what I had to say. I had nothing to say, as I was busy observing what was happening first. Because the old man sensed my gazing with intent, he decided to take his time. He started touching the car; first the front lights, using his index finger slightly raised above the surface, while the other fingers were pressed firmly on the metal. Then he walked around the car, caressing it dearly, his fingers on it almost making a perfect circle. 'Ah, yes,' he would then say with dreamy eyes, 'when this car took me all the way up to Grossglockner on the Austrian high alpine road, it gave me such a sense of freedom. And then Paris… This car gave me so many good memories. I took such good care of it too.' The circle was now almost complete. Mother didn't want him to finish his story, because she could sense what was going to happen next, so she intervened: 'I can see that you took good care of the car. I promise to cherish it as well,' she said, handing the man the signed registration. The man's finger reached the starting point, and it was now flashing in her direction. 'Listen, you know what, I'm not sure I want to sell this car. I'm 83. I don't need any money. I can just come in here, in the garage, and remember the good times. I'm sorry. The deal is off.' We were sorry too. That was so close.

We came home without the car. Mother asked me afterwards: 'what did you make of all that?' I said to her that I didn't like it one bit when the old man starting touching the car the way he did, as it pointed towards an old love affair hard to break. 'Yeah', she said. 'Too bad for us. We came so close.' Such is the nature of regret. In hindsight I think that this incident made me ponder on the greatest threat in the Bible embedded in the prophesy about what will happen to most who walk the narrow path to heaven. They come close to the gate, and yet they don't get to enter. I'm not sure that the fear of hell can beat the feeling of your heart sinking. You do your part, you're even more interesting than the ones who walk on the broadway, as you take up all the challenges of limitation, you come to the gate, you knock, you feel the heat of excitement in your knuckles, and then you just stand there, staring, for you realize that the gate will never open. You might as well turn back. But how? Just what metaphor can you think of that will save you from the turmoil in your heart?

Once I came across a Japanese phrase in free Google translation involving the concept of *kokoro*: 'the passion is boiled in the heart,' it said. I remember that this image lingered in my vocabulary for a long time. It must be the passive construction of it, as we're not here with the idea of hot passion, but with its alchemy. Imagine to be able to have agency over your passion, boil it, cool it, extract its essence, cook it and serve it as a magical potion. Every time I see a Fiat 500 I think of how the old man cast his own circle of protection in the name of this alchemy, the well-cooked bond between him and the car. No witch was going to take that from him, however well intended.

Touch is complicit with our acts of vision. When Romeo decided against selling his car to Juliet because of the stories of what he had experienced in the car, one could clearly see that his memories were not embodied by his visual remembrance, however vivid, but rather, by his touch. Sometimes I think of what might have happened if mother had offered herself to this old Romeo's touch, made a bold move towards breaking the line of his circle, so that instead of metal all the way through, his finger might have gone across her body. Alas, while mother may have been a genius, she was no cunning Juliet. Also, since her own desire was mediated by mine, as *I* wanted the car much more than she did, it afforded me no position to negotiate. The 83-year-old was not dealing with the 13-year-old, though it could have been interesting to see what strategy I might have come up with that would have barred the man from his refusal. My misfortune at the time was to be possessed by the demon of impossibility. I was not old enough and I had no control over money. I might have been able to seduce the old man, but that alone would not have cut it. Magicians of old had this notion that in order for any magic to succeed, three things must align perfectly. You can't put things in motion if you only control one variable, or if you only have access to half the platform for your actions.

When I read cards for a troubled Romeo and Juliet I try to identify what each can negotiate with. I look for symmetry in their relationship. Who gives what to the other, and how is it received? If reciprocity is not present, there's conflict. War. Sun Tzu in his influential *Art of War*, dating back to the 5th century BC, wrote that all warfare is based on deception. I think of all great love affairs as a battlefield. It is both impossible and unthinkable that either Romeo or Juliet doesn't have a winning strategy. Without the assumption that the battlefield is up for conquest, there's no love. But deception is part of it. Before I even put any cards down for it, I often ask the person in love: 'how do you deceive your lover? What is your winning strategy?' This is a counter-intuitive question, as lovers don't think in terms of deception when they want to conquer the other. But let me ask: would one not have to turn oneself into a demon, if the conquest of the other must be accomplished? Although I don't always say it to them, I read the cards for lovers in order to identify their demons, what demons they are possessed by, and what demons they think with. In this sense I'm not your regular fortuneteller, though I would stake my head on it that what we all do when we read the cards is enter the territory of deception, the Devil's domain.

'Does she love me, though?' Romeo insists on knowing, his eyes curiously piercing through the cards, and I often want to send him with his head into Juliet's bosom, rather than give him an answer. If he could deem that time stood still for both of them, then he would know, for Juliet can only touch him in one way that would disclose her bounty as boundless as the sea, her love as deep. While the cards can touch your desire in its visual manifestation, the physical touch can make you fully imagine the world of the boundless and deep love. A combination of the two, cards and touch, plus luck cuts the deal. If her deception was perfect, even a Juliet invested in speed and the promise of flight could take her new car for a spin and complete for herself her own magic circle and racing track.

Hard rain

Juliet is a poet in the great Romantic tradition, but what she really likes is math. She can't get enough of complex analysis, set theory, and the numbers whose infinity line is longer than that of any other numbers. Juliet is not a competent mathematician, but somehow she figured out that nothing is more romantic than the so-called real numbers. 'You're not ready for this,' she told Romeo, the minute his heart was beginning to pound to a soundtrack that she recognized as odd. Romeo's heart had a rhythm that matched hers. That was rare. Unique, actually. 'I'm ready,' he said, but he wasn't.

On occasion, when Juliet decides to have more dead men riding with her in her car, she asks Ayrton Senna to make space for Georg Cantor. When she handles the shift stick buttons in her red Mini Cooper S Coupé for real, she is ready for an outbound flight. She needs a mathematician on board for the hard rain.

The cognac magician

SOMETIMES LOVE IS ONE-SIDED. This is not exactly your classic Romeo and Juliet story, with both sharing a complete understanding of the lightning that strikes them. Sometimes it's only Romeo who gets hit, leaving Juliet in a state of wonder: 'what is wrong with you, man?' when the proper advances are made. Though, a perceptive Juliet would not need to ask that question. She may show regret in recognizing how pitiful it must be for the man to be in love with someone dedicated to another, or simply be in love with someone who doesn't care for him 'in that way,' meaning, the way devoid of the basic sublime experience of love, if, indeed, the sublime is ever subject to such classification. For what would be basic about the sublime? Nothing.

Once I returned to the city I grew up in, a military base in Romania where I lived between the age of 2 and 9. After my father died when I was 8, we moved to the place I was born in, but every once in a while I went back to visit the city of my early memories. I liked this city for its nature. A hefty river ran through it, and there was a spot there that had a marvelous beach. Nothing was better than to go swimming in this river during summer. For such an occasion I designed a special swimming suit, following all the rules of sympathetic magic you could think of. My two pieces had to match the spirit of the river. The fabric was green featuring a minimal design in the form of discrete yellow flowers. I decorated the top and bottom with an extra layer that I shredded, so that the strips would curl up, sending whoever gazed upon the construction to the image of the jungle or, even better, to Josephine Baker's famous banana skirt. It was perfect. I would take a dive in the river, and the 'bananas' would come up floating before I would emerge from the water, as if announcing a grand show. The local boys were mesmerized.

I was 17 at the time and I already knew a thing or two about how Eros works. The reason why I knew that I knew was in the proof of it. I would get invitations for sweets and drinks at the local hip place where lovers would gather. Once one of the boys was very insistent. But as he was not entirely dumb, he quickly understood that I was not the dating type. So he pulled all sorts of seduction tricks on me, especially the literary kind. He noticed what books I was reading by the river. I appreciated his effort and devotion. The only trouble was with the weather. His love was thunderous, but since lightning only hit him, I had issues with rising to his barometer. The hotter he got, the colder I got, and there wasn't a thing he could do about it. He learned, though, that I had a subscription to the opera house in the city he was living in, and made me promise to meet him before such a performance, just for a drink.

I promised that I would. Since I'm the type who keeps her promises, it wasn't long before I found myself in Romeo's city. I called him up and asked him out. He was faster than light.

We went to a place he recommended. We had the famed Romanian cake called *Diplomat* and cognac. It may have been Hennessy. I can't remember this part. Then he said: 'watch me go out of this place without paying the bill.' I was horrified, but I honored his request, as it was important for him to demonstrate something. He called the waitress and he praised her service. Then he said something about horrible weather, and how this place sheltered him whenever he got caught in a blizzard. He put his blazer on, while still maintaining eye contact, and then made a sign that I should do the same. We walked out without paying the bill. As he insisted that the whole treat had to be on him, including the deception, I didn't make any move myself towards paying, in spite of my indignation. Then he asked me: 'how did you like that?' I acknowledged his magician skills and we conversed on the topic of the power of suggestion. I did say to him, however, that if we ever met once more, he should never pull this trick on me again.

Then horrible weather actually also happened. We got caught in the worst, heavy rain that I had ever experienced. In a manner of minutes we got soaked to the bones. Romeo suggested that we went to his place that was right on the plaza we found ourselves in. This meant that I was going to meet his folks, as he still lived with his parents. How embarrassing. But what to do? I couldn't go home, requiring a one-hour train trip, in clothes that were sticking to my body. I accepted the solution, and I hurried to grab a huge bouquet of flowers on the way for his mother, as I could already visualize her performing magic on my dress. She was most kind. Excited too, as she assumed I was her son's secret lover. He had suggested this much to her. I wasn't surprised he did, as Romeo was invested in what he referred to as the 'suggestive sublime,' playing with risk and images of the risqué. After his mother ironed my dress and straitened its pleats, I bid them all farewell.

I never saw the man after this incident, as it was clear to him that what he dreamed of lacked symmetrical power. 'You don't think it would happen for you?' he asked me, referring to the possibility that I might turn one day into Shakespeare's Juliet. I assured him that it was not going to happen. I pointed to the clearing sky. There was no lightning in sight.

NOT READY

'You're not ready.' This is a line I often deliver to both men and women when they happen to act towards love on a false premise. As basic logic instructs that a false start leads to a false outcome, we don't even need a visual narrative with the cards in order to imagine just what acting out of a compromised love means. It means disaster. Replacing what we normally think is unconditional love – when lightning hits us in all the right places – with conditioned love – when love is based on acting for a good cause – leads to disaster.

Sometimes I read the cards for divorced men with children. 'I'm ready for a new relationship,' they say with confidence, and look to some guidance from the cards that might save them the trouble of engaging with 'the wrong woman again.'

In such cases, what is feared the most is the repetition of falling out of grace and the experience of everybody suffering, from the small family unit to the extended family and friends. While readiness to move on, as it were, may indeed be the case, the bizarre thing is that often the cards insist that the opposite is the case, suggesting that the time to mend has not been observed properly. 'So,' I ask the men I read for, 'you're ready to marry this other woman because you think that she will be a good mother for your child?' 'Yes, exactly,' they respond enthusiastically, when they see their cards and think that the trio, King of Batons, 6 Cups, and the Page of Coins, I point to sounds like a sweet deal, because 'it's in the cards.'

I often think about the second Juliet who thinks she will be first. I think about her readiness to enter the 'sweet deal' for the sake of motherhood, childrearing, or because saving the man she loves from the heartache inflicted by the first Juliet is a cause worthy of her love. I hear a storm coming and the voice of Romeo, troubadour Bob Dylan: 'A hard rain's gonna fall.'

What is missing from this string of cards here is the man's actual motivation to marry the woman he has in mind simply because he fell for her. Make that a hard falling too as this is *the* condition for curing the first love, for, as I said before, only a greater love can cure a failed, yet grand love. But some men insist that they don't want to go through *that* again, as if love itself is the problem. Thus there's almost no end to the number of false correlations that a disappointed heart can make. The King of Batons can take the path of pleasure again, but what is the real aim here? To please the enterprising child, the missing woman from the equation, or the string of cards on my table? I imagine Romeo going through the vows a second time around, saying to Juliet: 'I take thee to be my lawfully wedded wife, the second best, deliverer of the promise to be a good mother for my child.' What do we make of this great romance? The second Juliet stands no chance to even seduce the man, for in his speech act he will have already disclosed that what the woman marries is an impenetrable wall.

When love is one-sided it leads to disaster, especially if the cultural consecrations are performed. But how many have the courage to go through the hell of sublime love, again and again and again, if, indeed, one is lucky enough to stumble over the greater love several times in a life time? And if that is not possible, then why not have the courage to abstain, tell the hopeful and well-intended Romeos and Juliets of the world that they are not going to perform well under the circumstances, when the other loves another?

Loving on principle is not an option, and while one may think that a non-symmetrical love relationship can cut it when acting in the name of a cause is used as displacement for what doesn't exist at the essential level, loving on principle kills the mood for just loving. In Shakespeare's play we have a clear indication of what happens when lovers place themselves in a defending position of their name, rather than act out of what their true hearts tell them. Juliet's first cousin Tybalt, a skilled swordsman, loses his life to Romeo, the consequence being the banishment of Romeo from the community. Tybalt, the Prince of Cats and quite the loose gun, challenges Romeo to a duel not because he loves Juliet, though that is implied too, but because Romeo loves Juliet. Enabled by the old family rivalry, it's convenient for him to play with the basic mechanism of desire and turn it into a cause that has nothing to do with actual love.

Psychologically speaking, we only desire something because others also desire it. Look at capitalism and the world of marketing. It's built on this principle alone. Going for what others desire, thus all too easily becomes part of acting in the name of a cause. Juliet didn't ask for a knight in shining armor to defend her name, but Tybalt took it upon himself to do so. His risk calculation may have been sound enough, giving his skills at fencing, but what he forgot to account for was his own luck that he didn't have. He lost his life, making Juliet lament, yet in a most intriguing and rational way:

> My husband lives that Tybalt would've slain, and Tybalt's dead that would've slain my husband. All this is comfort. Wherefore I weep then? (3.2)

Indeed, for what reason must Juliet weep, when, in effect, balance is restored? Going to war with love itself, or the love that the heart knows beyond boundaries and limitations – moral codes and honor are such – is a lost cause. When our Juliet fails to know, or at least acknowledge the true heart of Romeo when she gives him her hand in marriage in exchange for her competence, rather than her love – that the man does not even seek – she steps into a battlefield whose outcome is already known to all war tacticians. In her calculations she may say to herself, 'maybe I get lucky, and Romeo will learn to love me,' but how likely will that be? When love is one-sided there can be no marriage arrangement without a thoroughly thought-out risk analysis. Even a hot-headed Juliet drunk on cognac can perform one such, but how often does she do it?

I read the cards for the Juliets who come to me to lament the situation that the Romeos I just mentioned in my example create, when they elect to displace their true hearts with another's desire. Sometimes children arrange the second marriage of their parents, because they can't bear to see them carry the burden of loneliness. I experienced this myself at close range. Although my mother was not the type who suffered from loneliness after my father died, as she had a rich life of the mind and did many interesting things as a result of it, my sister insisted that she got married again. Mother never did, and this left my sister in a perpetual state of wonder, 'what if she did, how might our lives have been transformed by another's love?' Personally I have to admit that I was happy that mother never gave in to that kind of curiosity, and continued to live her life spontaneously. She figured that if the greater love after my father was going to happen, she was going to take it from there. It never did, however, and she was fine with it. Seeing how a strong person had the bold resolve to either say yes to a greater love or, in its absence, simply abstain from engaging the heart, was a valuable lesson. I cherish the memory of it.

Ultimately it comes down to what knowledge we all possess. If we happen to know that some infinities are longer than others, we won't be stepping in any church giving our hands in marriage to the ones who can only promise us the shorter infinity line, the greater love still being reserved for another. What would be the purpose of it, we ask, especially since lovers want to know, 'can this love go all the way?' Sometimes I wish that when lovers come to me to ask this very question, they would also be in possession of what 'love all the way' means. Most don't. What they know is fear. As lovers often feel anxious about the possibility that time might fail them, thinking of the many divorce stories happening right after the marriage, they commit the fallacy of equating time — 'but for how long will he love me?' — with space, or the idea of 'all the way' covering a whole amorous territory that they all want to sit sovereignly in control of. In the story of 'love all the way' there's no space for second Juliets or Romeos who want to do the right thing by their kin. 'Love all the way' means exactly that, love all the way on the fearless path. A symmetrical love is not a love that shares different time lines or space lines. A symmetrical love is equally long and equally timeless. Who can step into it? Not many, alas, therefore the compromise.

If too late to remedy the compromise or avoid making it altogether, the consequence being that in spite of the fading religious feelings the churches are always full and ready for the 'forever' commitments, the cards can have theirs to say. 'Weep no more, sweet Juliet,' I say to the one who can't find comfort in her miscalculation. 'The cure for love is a greater love. Leave Romeo to his memories, because no matter how sharp your sword is, it will never be able to make the pendulum swing back to the time when you thought your love was great enough to make an impact, and be greater yet. If his love can't match yours, then all is lost to a vow without a heart in it.'

When the Hanged Man appears, it announces a situation that I like to identify as an event that can't be helped. The Queen of Swords may be able to act, justify her actions, and even show regret for the situation that can't be helped, but if the one she's up against is the Fool, then little can be redeemed. Usually fools are grateful to the ones who take them in and show them mercy in spite of their shortcomings, but are they what in popular parlance is called 'relationship material?' They are not. I don't even say this because it's easy to throw in the stereotype of the fool that can't be trusted, for, indeed, what has the idea of 'love all the way' got to do with trust? Nothing at all. The problem with fools is not their untrustworthy nature, but rather, the fact that they lack proper motivation. This doesn't sit well with the suit of warriors. The woman of the sword wants to know what she charges against, as a sense of movement and momentum is her livelihood. Without this sense there's no direction. Without this sense there's only an inappropriate mixing of metaphors, spatial and temporal, poetic and prosodic.

In Shakespeare's play, while Romeo and Tybalt can swing the iron swords, Juliet uses her tongue to fence with, demonstrating just how powerful an oxymoron can be. When she refers to Romeo having killed Tybalt as being a 'beautiful tyrant' and a 'fiend angelical' (3.2), she does more than put incongruent words together. There's calculated measure in her versification and an unambiguous sense of precision in hitting the target, for Romeo is *exactly* like that. Can a fool match such skills? If yes, the contract marriage has a chance to survive. If Romeo and Juliet marry their second best in relation to their true hearts' desires, then they have to make up for it one way or another. The bad news is, however, that what we refer to as 'one way or another' is in fact quite singular in its manifestation. There's only one way, not another, and that is the way of forgetfulness. If the first Juliet is not entirely forgotten about, she will be worse than a vampire, demanding the blood of the innocent bride as payment for making her love memorable.

The eleventh gate

When Romeo gazes upon Juliet, she is very particular about identifying what the intensity of his look unlocks. That's because Romeo doesn't gaze like that on anyone else. This gaze has to do with the gates of heaven. The eleventh gate, to be more precise.

'The eleventh?' Romeo asks her curiously, secretly wondering why Juliet isn't saying anything about the ninth gate. Since there's a text in women that only the Devil can read, Romeo figures that this gate of seduction is already open in his eyes. But Juliet knows him better than he knows himself. While she also likes occult movies in which the protagonist is Lucifer or some other high-ranking Demon, she prefers the cloak and dagger theme. Why stop at the ninth gate when you can go all the way to the eleventh, the invisible way?

Juliet takes Romeo's gaze and fastens it to her belt. She is ready to give him a meta-tour in his own mirrors.

Thresholds

OFTEN LOVERS NEED A COUNSELOR who is expert at conflict resolution. They go into therapy and get prompted to reflect on some set questions. When the questions fail to elicit the right answers, they come to me, the fortuneteller. I'm an expert at conflict resolution too, and I also prompt people to reflect on questions. But my questions never start with, 'what would make you a greater lover?' or 'when was the last time you really listened to your partner?' I may cast the cards for this question, 'how do you see me in this relationship?' that lovers insist on asking, assuming that it's necessary to lay down the ground for how they each can contribute to the wellbeing of the relationship. But what I like the most is when the cards refuse to give a standard and predictable answer, often of this nature: 'I'm going to cook for my wife every Tuesday and Thursday while listening to her needs, so that she won't have to be so stressed about putting me on the spot or having to do everything herself, and *that* will make me a greater lover.' There's nothing wrong with this resolve, other than the fact that it isn't terribly exciting.

In my experience, when Romeo and Juliet complain about troubles, I often see that the root of their grief has to do with the fact that they lost the plot of passion. Sometimes they can also see that, and yet, when it comes down to answering the question of how one can be a better lover, I note that they urgently try to find a solution in the form of some concrete pragmatism of the mundane kind. The mundane is great, but boring as hell if only internalized as a form of honoring what is basically an obligation. But passion knows no obligation. Passion finds some interesting thresholds to cross that have little to do with a constructed notion of the human imagination. And the mundane can be about many more things than the clichés about cooking or listening to the other, mainly because some therapist thinks it's a good idea. Once a woman got the Magician, 10 Batons, and the Ace of Batons.

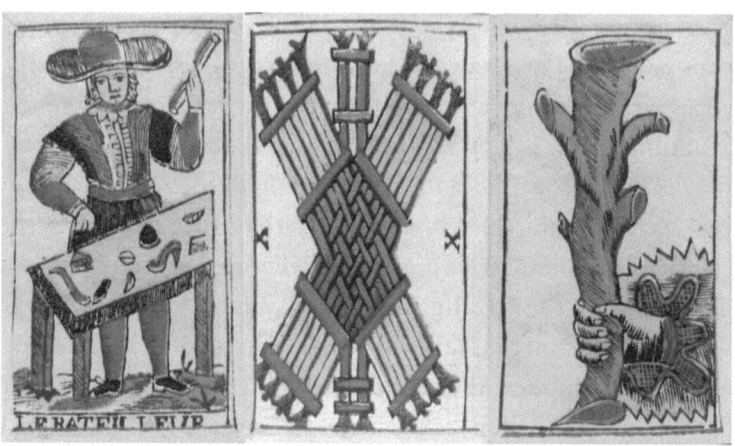

I asked the woman: 'when was the last time Romeo opened the eleventh gate for you?' She was taken aback by this question, and wanted me to elaborate. So I did. I asked her again: 'when was the last time Romeo told you that all he wanted from you in this relationship was for you to allow him to just look at you, gaze upon you with a most extraordinary intensity, one that goes even beyond the dazzling gate of seduction to the place where it captures the depth of your soul and wonder?' 'Ah,' Juliet said. 'Romeo never did that.' 'Why not?' I asked her in return. 'Are you not incurably in love?' The woman then pondered this question, and said: 'I don't know, maybe not. I think that what we both wanted to know in the beginning was how to take it to the next level.' 'What was this *it*?' I then asked her: 'Was this *it* not your great passion for one another, the sublime romantic expectation that whatever you did, the last thing you wanted from one another was to have expectations?' 'I'm afraid we didn't think in those terms,' Juliet then said, impatiently almost wishing that we somehow went back to the cooking and better listening idea.

But I'm relentless. In conflict resolution strategies, unless a threshold is crossed, there is no experience of the higher ground, or passing through the eleventh gate that gives people access to how they can perceive one another as art, to how they can understand that the only way to escape guilt and regret in a relationship is precisely if they see one another through art. That's why gazing is important. How do we gaze on the lover? What gates of heaven do we open when we do that? These are the questions to ask, as they have more potential to be of actual use than the ones that instill more guilt and more regret in lovers who wish to do better. When lovers go, 'I'm sorry, my dear. I should have listened to you more,' they perpetuate the guilt and regret that they ought to escape.

When Romeo and Juliet lack the ability to understand what their emotional and intellectual range consists of, how far it stretches, and to what extent it can be expanded without the ensuing feeling of guilt conditioned by culture, usually manifest in the exclamation: 'my god, I've just transgressed orders!' (tradition, rules, morality, or some other idiotic constraints that have nothing to do with what we could experience, if we saw past ideologies that cannot even legitimate their own existences), what they lack is an understanding of how to completely capture the other's attention. The greatest seduction is in this capturing of the lover's attention. When the other is incapable of ignoring you because of your enchantment, you bet that listening will happen, cooking will happen, and the fetching of the kids will happen. All without a sense of obligation, guilt or regret.

THE HOLE IN THE HEART

Juliet has not seen Romeo in eleven years. 'Does he still think of me?' she wants to know, and the cards say yes. Juliet's heart is like the hanging garden of Babylon, one of the seven wonders of the world. Although there are ancient written accounts of just what this garden looked like, since it is the only wonder among the seven in the world whose location has not yet been verified, the garden remains mythical in the human imagination. We can just see queen Semiramis, who supposedly ruled Babylon in the 9th century BC, tending to this garden, filling her eyes and heart with its beauty. Were there secret flowers in it? A rare black tulip perhaps?

The Devil initiating the string of cards here holds a tulip in his hand. Is Romeo still thinking of Juliet, whom he hasn't seen in eleven years, because of the magic of this flower, Juliet's favorite? It seems that insofar as Romeo gives as much attention to Juliet as she does to him, he tends to her garden, his gaze feasting on its wonders. 'What you cultivate grows,' the sages say, subtly hinting to the idea that the heart itself is a hole craving constant filling. Imagine pouring the content of the whole 9 Cups into the hole of the heart's desire. Not a small thing. 'Then what?' Juliet wants to know. 'Then nothing,' I tell her. 'You haven't seen Romeo in eleven years and and he hasn't seen you in eleven years, so things are as they are.' 'But will this change?' Juliet wants to know also on behalf of her mirror, Romeo. 'Who's to say?' I dreamily say, thinking of how we're still searching for Semiramis' garden.

There's architectonic knowledge that goes into this search, perhaps of the same proportion that distance has in relation to intimacy. Although counter-intuitive, it is distance that creates the greatest intimacy. Romeo and Juliet need not be in close proximity for the intensity of their gazing upon one another to create the reality of what each fills the hole of their heart with. What fills this hole is the image that each has of the other. Let's recall here the work of Jean-Luc Marion, and refer to a passage from his *Prolegomena to Charity* on the intentionality of love:

> Of the face offered to my gaze I envisage only what cannot be seen in it – the double void of its pupils, this void that fills the least empty gaze imaginable – because if there is nothing to see *there*, it is *from there* that the other takes the initiative to see (me). Gazing on the other as such, my eyes in the black of his own, does not imply encountering another object, but experiencing the other of the object. My gaze, for the first time, sees an invisible gaze that sees it. I do not accede to the other by seeing more, better, or otherwise, but by renouncing mastery over the visible so as to see objects within it and thus by letting myself be glimpsed by a gaze which sees me without my seeing it – a gaze which, invisibly and beyond my aims *(invisablement)*, silently swallows me up and submerges me, whether I know it or not, whether or not I want it to do so (Marion, 2002: 82).[1]

As mentioned before, most fortunetellers tend to dismiss the question of whether a distant lover is still thinking of the other, especially if a considerable number of years have passed since the two had an encounter. But what has time to do with the intensity of an image? If Romeo holds Juliet's image vividly in his mind, filling the hole of his heart with it, then that image is his reality. As such, it will appear in the cards, as the cards have a ludic way of insisting that this is the case. 'Yes, but does it go anywhere?' the pragmatists want to know, yet the answer to this question is not found in relating this image to movement and direction, but rather in relating the image to the gate of the highest imagination where we find it. This is good enough for most, especially since, on occasion, it makes lovers don their fetish shoes, whose magic can bring them to the feet of the other. Romeo can kneel and kiss the hem of Juliet's silver gown, because once he can imagine the very thing, he will find the proper channel to manifest his desire.

THE SOUND OF TWO RED SHOES CLAPPING

In 2001 I attended a Wagner performance of *Tristan and Isolde* at Carnegie Hall in New York under the direction of Daniel Barenboim. Waltraud Meier and Nadja Michael were singing in the main roles. I can't remember who performed in the role of Tristan, as I ended up filling my heart, eyes, and ears with the presence of another Romeo sitting right behind me. He was a very restless gentleman and completely infatuated with Nadja Michael's stage presence. Up until that point I had never experienced sitting next to someone whose body language could speak equally as powerfully as a Wagner soprano. He wore expensive red shoes and a striped petroleum color suit. Impeccable attire, no doubt carefully thought about in terms of guessing what Michael was going to wear: a lavish fat silk silver gown. He got it right. Perfect match. When the concert was over he almost got himself arrested, as he jumped over Barenboim and nearly dragged Michael off the stage. She was taken aback by his violence, but at the same time it was clear that she was also very flattered.

The image that stayed with me over the years was that of his red shoes. To this day I still wonder what Devil he must have been possessed by, as the stunt that he pulled was close to the impossible, speaking from the point of view of what is physically feasible. All I can remember is the sound of his shoes cast forcefully forward and almost touching my ears. I was sitting in the front row just behind the conductor. In order for Romeo to get to his Juliet, he had to go over the heads of the people in front of him, and then past the conductor's baton. He had interminably long legs, and they were doing all the action, completely overmatching Barenboim's baton. There was a clear rhyme here between long objects, between the legs and the baton, with only color marking a difference. The man's red shoes were more striking than the mahogany color of the conductor's baton. I perceived this whole scene as a duel. When he got to the stage, he grabbed Juliet's gown and kissed it, before he let his long body emerge in its full height, his arms grabbing the woman by her waist. He lifted her up and then carried her towards the exit. The security guards intervened, and rescued the singer from this outburst of passion.

No one knew who this man was, nor what his intention was. People were whispering displaying the face of horror in their voices: 'what does he want, is he a terrorist?' I almost wanted to join the choir, yet sing a song of my own in counterpoint: 'isn't it clear what he wants? He wants her, the woman.' I then tried to imagine just what image of the singer this Romeo must have had in his head, when he decided to plot her abduction. The flowers also gave away the intentionality of his love. I'm not sure I'd seen a more elaborate bouquet. Red roses. Hundreds of them. I couldn't even begin to imagine where he kept them. Were the flowers under his seat? How was this possible, given their volume? But the flowers explained why I got to see and hear the red shoes first. When the man cast his legs over the front row, the rest of his body was busy with holding on to the flowers.

I'm quite convinced that on that day the law of gravity was suspended. Now I wonder if Nadja Michael went home that night, and intoned to Shakespeare's balcony scene: 'O Romeo, Romeo, wherefore art thou Romeo?' The red shoes Devil exposed himself to her, laid himself open outside all visible sensibility, demonstrating responsibility for the image he had in his mind. While the work of a madman, he enjoined Juliet out of a purely romantic obligation that imposed itself on him and that was constituted by something other than even his own intentionality. What is most surprising, really, is that somehow no one ever thinks that love is not only violent and transgressive, but also pathological. When I go to a wedding, I always try to imagine what goes on in the lovers' heads when they follow the procession and orderly say their vows. I never hear the violent call of the black tulip or the transgressions of the reddest of the red roses in their voices, but shouldn't this very call be the most visible threshold here?

Satisfaction

'I can't give you the satisfaction of knowing what's in my heart,' Romeo tells Juliet in reference to admitting to what he already disclosed, the wrenching passion in his heart. 'But you laid it open to me,' Juliet says, thinking about the logic of not giving satisfaction when satisfaction was served on the first heart beat. Why would Romeo think that she forgot the sound of that? 'Perhaps you're right,' Romeo says, and Juliet loses her patience: 'You're damn right that I'm right.'

Romeo may be a skilled swordsman, but Juliet knows that if she ever had to demand satisfaction, duly challenging Romeo to a duel, she would kill him on the first blow. A Romeo who speaks in the tentative language of the 'perhaps' is no match for her. She was trained by three musketeers and four samurai. When she wields the sword, she wins. She decides to write a poem instead about rage, hunger, and the softest glove slapping the cheek.

The Knights Templar

PART OF MY ACADEMIC LIFE when I was a professor at Roskilde University consisted of going to conferences. Once I was in Köln hanging out with literature lecturers, psychoanalysts, and artists. With a few friends we took a tour of the Dom, the magnificent cathedral from 1242 that is a close imitation of the one in Amiens. As with cathedrals of this caliber, the legend has it that the first architect made a pact with the Devil, so that the construction would be unique and hold the ones entering it under a spell. I always think of pacts and what we use them for. If this is true indeed, then what the architect made a deal for was how to encode the language of the birds, or the power of the oracular into the stones.

    The night before the tour of the Dom I read the tarot cards for my friends over beers and weird light at the local pub. Three of the four I was with were like the three musketeers. Rainer Kaus, a Kafka specialist and psychoanalyst, was always accompanied and attended to by two of his PhD students, a man and a woman. The man had a question for the cards that was about doubt and ambivalence: should he continue with his Jesuit studies or do philosophy instead? I cast the cards to get an insight into an alternative reality. As it happened, the cards fell precisely into place reflecting the nature of his question. He got the Lovers, the Hermit, and Justice.

I told him to go with philosophy. The morning after, while we were all looking at some detail art in the cathedral, he told me how, on the way back to his hotel room around midnight, he heard the organ playing very loudly in this very place. There were no lights on, and there was no traffic around. It was all very quiet except for the music thundering all of a sudden. 'My god,' I said to him, feeling jealous: 'you heard the language of the birds. How fortunate.' He wanted to know what the meaning of it was, and I told him again to go with philosophy. A Jesuit would not need to ask the question about meaning.

Then, while looking at the beautiful stained glass windows from the Renaissance, depicting what we often find in the tarot cards, I initiated a number of other people visiting the Dom into the legend about the nomadic cathedral, the tarot cards. With the destruction of the Order of the Temple on the night of October 13, 1307, the masons and the architects of the sacred buildings went underground. Their teachings re-emerged, however, around 1400 in Northern Italy. The legend has it that in order to prevent the assassination of the masters who opposed the dogmatic system at the time, all the knowledge they had about how the sacred can be experienced literally and in a direct way, should be encoded unto a pack of cards. The Knights Templar were entrusted with this pack, and they were to guard it with their games. What would be a better place to hide a secret knowledge than in plain sight? Considered a tool for games, the pack of playing cards with the added tarot trumps provided a perfect cover for this effort. Even now some historians of the occult look at a tarot pack with this in mind, that is to say, with the desire to decode what the masters of old supposedly encoded in these cards, from knowledge of the self to the architectonic structure of the soul.

Everyone listening to me liked this idea. We then split with the larger group and came out of the Dom, thinking of what else we should see. The three musketeers decided that since our morning was an obvious continuation of the theme of tarot and cathedrals that started the evening before, we should stick to churches. Rainer suggested that we all went and saw another master, an art therapy professor, painter, and a hardcore Lacanian. He literally lived in a church. A modern church, but a church nonetheless. At some point, when the catholic congregation in his neighborhood went over to graze on other pastures, the man bought the place and turned it into an art gallery. He himself lived in the bishop's rooms right across the main building. The altar was kept in his living room and filled with postcards of the man's paintings, all featuring variations over Gustave Courbet's *L'Origine du Monde*, the famed depiction of a woman's sex. Rainer's friend never painted anything else. For him *that* was the Real, the place between the legs of the woman we all came out of. We sat like that in wonderment in the middle of the Real and drank a *grand cru* French wine, while stuffing ourselves with goat cheese and Danish cookies.

 The artist wanted the failed Jesuit and soon-to-be consecrated philosopher to read some fragments. He picked Hölderlin, whose difficult syntax, yet very lyrical falling tone created a mood of gravity. We all felt pulled towards the stone, the altar piece dedicated to the origin of the world. We said to the man who couldn't be a Jesuit that this was his last chance to act as one. Hell, we even decided to raise him in rank. He could be a Cardinal giving us a blessing. He felt a relief when we didn't propose the Pope. I had a simple explanation for it, since it was my idea to switch vocations and ranks in the first place. In Alexandre Dumas' cloak and dagger bestselling series of novels, based on the life and times of valiant swordsmen, the three musketeers never had any dealings with the Pope. They tried to outwit the clever Cardinal Richelieu instead, sometimes with dire consequences. We got a very soothing blessing. Courbet was winking in the wings, and we all felt that we simply knew what there was to know.

We left this cathedral in Rainer's vintage 1980 blue Mercedes. While cruising through the woods, Rainer's queen student, *Die Köningin,* was trying to communicate to us what the plan was. This woman was used to getting things done. But Rainer turned on the music instead and said: 'here's the short version of what the meaning of life is: spend your time wonderfully.' Thus spoke the oracle. Barbra Streisand got channeled and we all marveled at her voice as it enforced Rainer's point. Her song *Woman in Love* made us all nod. And I was thinking: this *is* the language of the birds. Sung in Rainer's blue cathedral and seen in Courbet's cathedral.

When Romeo and Juliet speak in the language of infinity with one another, ambivalence and doubt dissolve. There is no *perhaps* here. Only, 'you're goddamn right that I'm right.' When the heart is penetrated to its deepest core, what's the point of denying having seen that, having felt it, having heard it, having smelled it, having touched it? When Romeo got speared by Cupid, the pink angel of love, he didn't say to his intended, 'I can't give you the satisfaction of knowing that I'm now in a secret cathedral, singing your praises with all the archangels.' Why are some Romeos afraid of this language? There's cliché and then there's the ode, a poem meant to be sung. 'So sing it, for fuck's sake,' I want to say to the Romeos who are stunned and fear that the right words won't come out, and in this fear they let all the wrong ones fall instead, as punishment for Juliet's ultimate sin, which is to know her lover's heart.

While cruising in a car that was not so fast Barbra Streisand offered us an ode that sings the praises of infinite love:

With you eternally mine
In love there is no measure of time.
We planned it all at the start
That you and I live in each other's heart
We may be oceans away
You feel my love, I hear what you say
No truth is ever a lie
I stumble and fall but I give you it all.

I am a woman in love and I do anything
To get you into my world and hold you within.

Being in the mood for love exceeds the purpose of it. Planning may be part of it, but living in each other's hearts has no other purpose than to be so. When lovers stumble in their relationship, it's often because they confuse their passion with purpose. Asking them about their passion is one thing. Asking them about their purpose is another. The first presupposes an awareness of *now* – it is *now* that I love. The latter is an illusion. While the purpose in life has always been physical – 'be fertile,' they all say, of the earth and women – passion is of another dimension. You can passionately declare that the purpose in life is to do the best you can right now. Try not to kill anybody, be too angry with idiots, leave grand legacies to your children, or think that just because things happen to you, they are significant. And then what?

If lovers relaxed about the purpose of their love in life, or the meaning of it, they might discover that they could be at peace with one another's eternal love. They wouldn't even have to entice one another to be better listeners, take the trash out more often, or presuppose that only the other gender is good at certain things. Sometimes Juliet is faster than Romeo with her guns and her cars. Will Romeo weep over this lamentable situation, because weeping is now in fashion? Some Juliets are not seduced by the trick called 'show me your vulnerability.' If Romeo has a good reason to weep, then he can do it in the from of an ode, one in which he praises Juliet's healing hand on his crotch, if that is where the pain is. If the hole in each lover's heart is filled by the other, listening is inherent, the real touching of the heart is inherent, and so are all the other acts that stem from paying attention, simply because one can't help it otherwise. If the other falters in his step, you give him your all. Such an attitude is not up for negotiation. You don't negotiate with what you claim is eternally yours. How could you?

PROTECTING WHAT'S MINE

If divination works wonders, it's because of the questions that people bring to the fortuneteller's table. But not all questions have the same, strong caliber. Some questions are weak, vague, incoherent, and imprecise. Other questions are downright wrong, even when they are well intended. Sometimes lovers ask this common question, 'how can I protect our love?' without thinking about what is presupposed here, namely a threat. But what kind of a threat? How visible is it? Or are we here with the intangible kind, often manifest in the form of an ominous feeling that something bad is going to happen?

Now, if this purported love is the kind I like to speak about, namely the kind that is utterly beyond all fear, then the question of protecting the love is already out of place. You don't protect that which protects itself. A love that's conscious of its form is not something that you protect. A strong love that knows its own justice is a love that can sit in the middle of the fire. It can burn with the fire, yet without clinging to the wood the way fire does. Such a love is not subject to the lover who lacks courage, the courage to see it for what it is without judgment, without evaluation, and without imposition.

In an analogy, imagine the declaration of love that Shakespeare's Juliet makes, when she refers to the boundlessness of her love. Now imagine Romeo saying to Juliet, 'I will protect this love.' What kind of arrogance would he be afflicted by in assuming that this boundless love is like some holy grail? There is no Knight Templar who can protect such a love, for its form is the formless.

Still, Romeo wants me to ask the cards about it. I cast them against my desire and discernment. Romeo gets these cards: Judgment, Force, and the Moon.

This is what I tell him: 'I can see that you want to protect the family grave, but which part of it is it that you don't get? Why are you forcing it? A love that is as boundless as the sea is not subject to protection. There is always another world that tends to it, a world that is beyond your dreams and the imagination. Your fear may sense this world, but this world is not your fear.' Romeo is not convinced, as he likes to insist. But for once, I tell him that I hate repeating myself. I send him to sit some more under Juliet's balcony, and heed her call. What exactly does he hear when she says, 'O Romeo, Romeo, wherefore art thou Romeo?' or when she invokes his presence by the power of the moon and the night:

> Lovers can see to do their amorous rites
> By their own beauties; or, if love be blind,
> It best agrees with night. Come, civil night,
> Thou sober-suited matron, all in black,
> And learn me how to lose a winning match […]
> Come, night; come, Romeo; come, thou day in night;
> For thou wilt lie upon the wings of night
> Whiter than new snow on a raven's back.
> Come, gentle night, come, loving, black-brow'd night,
> Give me my Romeo; and, when he shall die,
> Take him and cut him out in little stars,
> And he will make the face of heaven so fine
> That all the world will be in love with night
> And pay no worship to the garish sun. (3.2)

If Romeo paid proper attention, he would hear in Juliet's discourse a refusal to translate love into the property of time.

All that is more

Juliet likes her balcony. It's made of glass and Brazilian walnut wood. For eternity. She figured that if Romeo would come climbing on it, he would inscribe his love on the wood. For eternity.

Juliet is smoking on her balcony, thinking of speed. What if the message about the other Juliet, Shakespeare's Juliet, had reached Romeo in time? What if Shakespeare had access to the literature of speed, something you find in **The Tale of Genji**, the first ever novel written by a Japanese Juliet, many centuries before Shakespeare made his mark?

Juliet is thinking of the time when only one Romeo in her life said this to her: 'if only I can be with you five minutes, then I can die happy.' She asked him in disbelief: 'Really? Then, you have no expectation?' 'I have none,' Romeo said. She understood that he trusted her. But what has trust got to do with love?

Death on wheels

Sometimes I think about why Shakespeare's Juliet killed herself. You'd think it's because of grief; because she couldn't bear the pain of her loss. When Romeo died because he thought she died, she thought she had to die too. For real. But what if she killed herself not because of grief, but because she couldn't plot a revenge? Often loss calls for revenge. Instead of grief, Juliet could have tried another emotion. Anger, for instance. How dare Romeo kill himself? Had Juliet been angry, she might have made something out of it. She might have avenged herself through words. She was good with words. But she chose to silence herself. Death was on a roll. Death was on wheels. Fast wheels. No one else would have Juliet. Only Romeo would have Juliet. And if Romeo couldn't have her in life, he would have her in death.

Possessiveness works with the economy of loss. We are possessive in love because we project the fear of losing the other to death or to another. When the vows in church are said and the words, 'until death do us part,' fall like a hammer, they nail a coffin. I wonder how many realize that when they say those words, what they do is not only consciously conjure death, but give it a task too. 'Roll,' they say, and before you know it, we're all in a Werner Herzog film featuring Romantic heroes pursuing impossible dreams, the highest aim of knowing the heart of man being reserved to the director. Why are lovers always at odds with the ways in which they try to consecrate their love through ritual? Why do they not understand that there's a discrepancy between what they vow and the very dream of the impossible they pursue? How many understand the implications of their own declarations? 'I love you, my love, with an infinite love,' they *all* want to say, and it gets even more interesting when the lover is a mathematician, as he might throw into his vow the specificity of just what infinity line his love situates itself on, when we're talking about integers and real numbers, as some infinity lines *are* longer than others. Imagine that!

On this, I have to admit that I like the irony in what we assume about mapping correspondences. Even though very few read Shakespeare, if you were to ask young couples in love about their loves, you'd be surprised at just how many would say that their love is something as strong as in Shakespeare's play *Romeo and Juliet*. Never mind that most don't even know what the play is about, but they heard that it's about the ultimate love, the love that went 'all the way.' This is fair, because it is so, but what are we to make of the couples who map their love unto Shakespeare's play, when nothing is actually known about what Shakespeare thought of it, the ritual marriage in particular? While there's a lot of fretting about it in the play, we never actually go through the 'death do us part' part. The friar agrees to marry the couple, and there's a lot of sending forth of each of the two to what Shakespeare calls 'the cell,' the friar's dungeon, this word conjuring already the notion that if the vows will be said, they will be said in secret and in a hurry too. Juliet never gets to put the ring on Romeo's finger either. She sends it forth to him through her nurse. So we're here with the circus of the marriage ritual, corrupted by the wrong setting and by time, as the two hardly have a minute for their saying yes to one another. And we never actually get to this yes. It's not written anywhere. There is no 'until death do us part.' How quaint of Shakespeare to leave all that out of his most famous play... Even though a Catholic phrase whose origin dates back to 1549, where we find it in *The Book of Common Prayer* as 'till death us depart,' as a ritualist playwright *par excellence*, Shakespeare could have chosen to move our hearts with it, when the play premiered in 1597, but he didn't.

I'd say that what Shakespeare did there was to distort the image of the sacred ritual on purpose in order to highlight the vehemence in evading what is redundant already, namely the actual consecration of the marriage through the stamp of societal approval. Let's just say that Shakespeare put a spike in death's wheels, when he depicted the fretting circus about the marriage ritual in the presence of the friar as a mirror to the marriage that took place under Juliet's balcony, in the presence of the lovers' hearts, when they both gazed into one another's abysses. And yet the image that persists throughout the ages is very much the image of 'I do' in its full church intangibility.

Because the general ignorance about the steps Romeo and Juliet take in order to consolidate their bond so amuses me, I've conducted a test myself on a private basis, as I'm always curious to know just what picture of love fills people's heads, when they liken their love to that of *the* Romeo and Juliet. What I found is that this image is not in the book, Shakespeare's book, that is. Rather, it's in people's own imagination of it as a fragment of their own self-fashioned desires.

Now, why this discussion here? Remember what I started out with? A scene in which Juliet number two acts on a false premise towards her marriage vows. She thinks that she is number one, the one and only in Romeo's heart, but if you asked Romeo about it, he would have to admit that although he's standing right there by the altar, committed to saying the words to the wrong woman, the love he has for Juliet number two is not exactly the same as the one he still entertains for another, the one he fell for before, hard and at first sight.

In my practice as a fortuneteller I read the cards for this situation, when I find that most of the work I must perform — when lovers present me with snakes in their imagined paradise — actually consists in defining the real basis for why the two have entered the marital institution. While love at first sight occurs all the time, it is not a given that marriage follows automatically. This often has to do with the non-availability, as it were, of the other, when either Romeo or Juliet is already given into marriage to another person, or have commitments that prevent them from showing up in church where they can consecrate their mutual love. But as other such commitments do not equal preventing the lovers from enacting the balcony scene, where eternal love can be declared, this means that what we're dealing with is uncorking the coffin. When lovers come to me and say, 'I've tried, but it doesn't work out because the other is still hung up on the past,' I cast the cards for the impossible situation. What do I then find?

A LOVE LESSON

When people come to me to hear about love, I regard their trust that I can offer something useful a high privilege, even though, personally, I regard trust as completely irrelevant to the work that I do. People ask a question and I answer it. Whether what I have to say is deemed trustworthy or not has nothing to do with the reality of what I see emerge from the cards and the images that I read. As I'm here to serve the purpose of answering a question, I don't make evaluative judgments, or take the others' evaluative judgments as a measure for what I'm about to perform. Therefore such divination sessions don't last long. If called for, before I even put any cards on my table, I may engage with a preliminary lesson in why the new love that has now turned to hatred doesn't work. This would be part of defining the premise for why the two married in the first place.

Here's what I say by taking into account the way people themselves invoke a time-frame for their narratives, based also on their desire to understand precisely 'what went wrong,' thus invoking as well a causal relation. First I break down the temporal dimension, and start making axiomatic sentences pertaining to the past, present, and future dynamics.

In the past: 'love was what it was. Nothing more, nothing less. If it didn't work out, it's because the two of you (and sometimes a third one involved) were not on the same page.

In the present: 'love is what it is. Nothing more, nothing less. If it doesn't work out, it's because the two of you (and sometimes a third one involved) are not on the same page.

In the future: 'love will be what it'll be. Nothing more, nothing less. If it won't work out, it's because the two of you (and sometimes a third one involved) will not be on the same page.

These declarative sentences are then followed by the observation that it is pointless to invent narratives that depict the other that one now hates in a colorful way, in a language that would make the distressed party feel better about themselves. Granted, there is 'coping with the situation' when the hated one is now referred to as being a liar, immature, unconscious, ungrateful, stupid, uneducated, insensitive, vain, narcissistic, hysterical, manipulative, or a witch. But love is still what it is, and the fact that the other may or may not be all these things is beside the point. If love doesn't work, it's because the parties involved are not on the same page.

Now to the art of it: 'what does being on the same page mean?' some ask. To this I ask in return: 'do you give all, or are you ambivalent? Does the other give all, or is the other ambivalent? If there's incongruence, then you can be sure that it won't work. Love is what it is. You can only give all, and think of the other as your first priority, not as an option.'

Finally I also offer the suggestion that outside of time/space constraints there is love that exceeds existence, the *is*. Here I add: 'blessed are the ones who know what that means.'

Once I read for a lover who could see the obvious in it. 'But this is death, isn't it, this sermon about being on the same page, because when does *that* ever happen?' Indeed. Death is on wheels, heading towards a crash. My lover querent here wanted to know if I ever came across a couple that managed to not exhaust their hearts. What was their secret?

I liked this question so much that I put the cards down for it. This was a question not only about how to grab a heart, but most importantly about how not to waste it. I shuffled my cards and marveled at the string on my table. The Charioteer, Death, and Justice showed up, instantly presenting me with a line that had a certain ring of urgency to it.

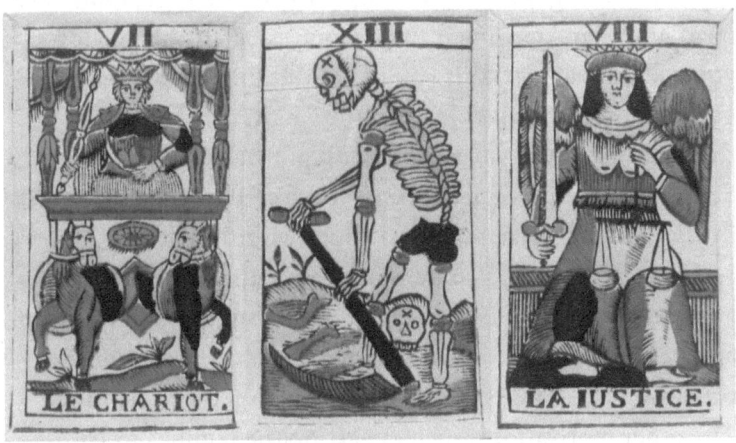

I offered this insight: 'the lovers who succeed in being on the same page, managing to conserve their hearts while burning them for one another, kindly stop for death and find truth.' Those familiar with the poet Emily Dickinson, a thinker who wrote in Shakespeare's vein, will recognize the twisting of her lines here:

> Because I could not stop for Death –
> He kindly stopped for me
> The Carriage held but just Ourselves –
> And Immortality. (Dickinson, 1976: 350)

In Dickinson's poem we find a voice of acceptance and gratitude. I'm not sure I understood myself what the line in my own head meant, when I suggested that the lovers who get it right do so because they 'kindly stop for death and find truth,' and I may have to reflect on this further, but one thing is certain: being on the same page with another, grabbing their heart and then knowing it fully, requires being able to stop yourself in your tracks. If you're not offering your lover your gaze that holds the whole of eternity in it, then stop right there and re-assess what you're doing. Just *look* at the other. Sense what the other needs. Can you feel what the other needs in your bones? Make that need your own true justice.

'That's a tall order,' some would say, failing to provide an argument for why it is so difficult to just stop and watch, stop and pay attention, stop and breathe the sweet breeze of the other's breath. This is what we call being on the same page. The other motivations, such as getting the families to approve of the union, getting the bank to approve of a loan for a dwelling, and getting the bosses one works for to approve of the maternity leave when that happens are aspirations that have nothing to do with knowing the heart of another. These are just societal goals and agreements.

Some lovers confuse these goals with their heart's true desire. Some convince themselves that these goals are the direct result of their heart's desire. But I beg to differ. I've seen too many lovers crash because the mappings of their constructed desires didn't correspond with the spontaneity of their hearts. While many invoke beauty in their justification for following the path of ritualizing the idea of love, marriage, children, and the happy family, an idea is still an idea, not the thing itself, or the reality of the heart. When it goes wrong for many couples, when the pages of their common script get mixed up, they find that they each read a different book. They forget to stop and look the other in the eyes, and ask directly: are we still reading the same book? What page are we on now?

What we also find of significance in Shakespeare's play, especially where getting a love lesson is concerned, is the idea of stopping for the sun and the moon, the stars, and stones. Both Romeo and Juliet have their mouths filled with nature. Recalibrating being on the same page can start with a consideration of the heart of nature. Is the pulse of the heart of nature clear? Stopping to listen to it is the same as kindly stopping for death, as the function of nature is to give us a lesson in how to survive. Observing what happens in nature confronts us with our mortality, as there's no bird or plant whose life is not either taken or given in exchange for another's life.

The function of the idea of being on the same page is to make us stop in our tracks and put us in a state of being at a loss for words. And breath. This is high art, because in this stopping, in the holding of our breaths, we forget about our cultural selves and existences. As a consequence, we can experience true beauty in the world. Indeed, to be able to kindly stop for death and find the truth in the beauty of knowing the heart of another is no small thing, as it requires both courage and a sense of singularity, the kind that has the power to grab your heart so you can exclaim to yourself: 'here's the whole universe in a single image, or a flower, or a color, or a line. And I like it. A lot.'

BEYOND GRIEF

A woman artist wanted to know how she could balance between what she herself called 'displacing acts.' She was in love with a man she couldn't be with due to circumstance. As a result, she would create a lot of art, write about it, and teach it to others too. While her heart was settled in these acts, she wanted to know if this was all. As Romeo was as real to her as she was to her own reality, this Juliet wanted to know what the nature of her so-called 'saving grace' was. She was a source of inspiration to others, in the process using her love and loss as her main fountain of creativity. But was she alright with using herself? Using the other? Or was their shared reality the only reality worth talking about?

I liked this series of questions as they were all related to form. What this Juliet wanted to know was *exactly* what form her love had. She had a clear sense of how it manifested, but what form did it have, essentially?

As it happens, what we call 'creative genius' often has to do with how we measure loss, writing being referred to by many as springing directly from a source connected to loss, with grief, anger, rage, and regret being chief manifestations of loss. Shakespeare's *Romeo and Juliet* play falls in the genre of tragedy. Tragedy establishes a direct lineage that connects loss, rage, grief, and regret. It's tragic when lovers split up, when one of them dies, or when they can't have one another for whatever reason.

Although each lover may experience their love and loss differently, essentially what we're talking about is the degree of awareness each brings to the table that informs the meaning of each individual emotion one goes through. Raging because you're grieving may not give awareness much space for internalizing how the movement from one state goes to another. That would require a distancing from the emotion, which would then bring about an awareness of how this emotion is put together, what gives it intensity, and how strongly it impacts on the memory that construes it to begin with.

Being able to distinguish between various states of emotions as they relate to forms of displacement is a high art already. Hence the existence of art. There's building out of grief, and then there's the scaffolding that moves the heart. We call the first coping. The second is art. As an example, we can ask, though: if writing displaces grief, painting displaces rage, or teaching displaces regret, then what? Could one work on these arts of inspiration and instruction without being assaulted by the strong emotions that prompts them? Could one sit in the middle of the fire, yet without clinging to the fire the way wood clings to it? I've offered this image right here before.

I had a feeling that when the woman posed her question about her work being a means of displacing her grief, what she also wanted to know was something about the ability to create without attachment to her memories. So now we throw fear into the premise for her question as well, for indeed, it's legitimate to ask: what would happen to the woman if she lost her loss, as it were, if her sense of this loss would suddenly vanish? What would happen to her project of honoring her love through her grief? And yes, we talk about a project, simply because any artist who uses distancing as a means to getting intimately close to the idea of knowing the heart and moving it too, consciously harmonizes her actions with a greater power, the power of allowing the other (love, loss, grief) to hold power over her imagination; thus an art project whose underlying structure is the approximation of beauty to the hardness of the emotion. Love is hard, and so is grieving over its loss.

Now, when I read the cards for situations such as these, when lovers go through the fear of losing twice, first the love and then its loss, I already have an eye prepared to see how the images of the tarot can implicitly address this very question, 'then what?' Is there a structural hierarchy in this question, 'then what?' that says something about the sequence in which going from love to loss is experienced? Is there a trumping force when we talk about rage, grief, and regret? Which one of these emotions is more intense or has more staying power? When we also talk about the fear of losing all these emotions, are we not talking about yet some other displacement of them, for how can the psyche ever forget anything?

With all this in mind, let us finally see what I said to the woman who wanted to know about the form of her love, and what she could make of her acts of displacing the emotions she went through, as she was experiencing the fear of losing them. Her desire was to keep going for the sake of her art. Her 'infinite love' was not put into question. Just her work. The cards were generous and clear in their message. The woman got the Sun, the Charioteer, and the Star.

We're with Romeo and Juliet brilliantly loving under the sun. A beautiful image. Romeo comes riding in his shining armor, while Juliet kneels in devotion, making her offering in the form of her naked self and the gifts she is able to pour out of her chalices. The form of this love is to give the other exactly what the other gives you. Even the two horses and the two containers in the Star's hands rhyme with the presence of the two in their private garden. The form of this love is like that of our closest star, Sol Invictus. Juliet knows of its power best, as above her eight other stars are in attendance. If Romeo is guided by his drive, Juliet is guided by celestial inspiration. If her love is a bounty as deep and boundless as the sea, it is because of the infinite sky. Who can count the stars? How long would that take?

Upon seeing these cards I asked the woman to think in all earnest whether she thought it was possible at all to lose such a love. 'It was not,' she said. What was lost about her love was the physical connection with the other, not the emotion. That one was as shiny and as bright as all the stars that led to the encounter in the first place. The issue here was not with the light, but with the momentum, being at odds with the other's timing. My Juliet's problem was similar to Shakespeare's Juliet's problem. If only Romeo had waited a few more minutes by her catafalque, he would have experienced Juliet rising up from the dead. But he couldn't wait. He killed himself before she could make her move. That was tragic. Could the woman I was reading the cards for continue to use Romeo's self-inflicted death as fuel for her drive, the urgency she felt to displace his death with her art? Although such a displacement presented itself to her vehemently, what was she to do in the face of constantly hitting the wall called *contretemps*, or wrong timing?

It was hard to find the words that could replace the light from so many stars in this string of cards. What can replace such light? The light is there, enhanced even, considering that we go from one bright star to eight of them, from the Sun to the Star, and Romeo is still out there riding, yet living a life parallel to Juliet's. Or was his Chariot heading towards her? In many interpretative renditions of the Star, we find this card associated with hope. Are we here with hope? The woman started with a question about consolation, or rather the inconsolable, for what was there to hope for in the face of loss? Too many paradoxes presented themselves here, the primary tension being between grief and hope. You can't grieve properly, if you're still hoping. So which one was it? Was Juliet still hoping, lending her grief this form, or was she just hoping, using the image of grief as a displacement for her hope? If she couldn't dare to hope, perhaps she was making space for grief, but grief refused to usurp the throne reserved for hope. Such is the work of resistance.

What the cards showed here was actually this unresolved situation between the state of declaring that all is lost and the reality of the opposite. All was not lost. The stars in the larger picture here showed 'all that is more.' I sent Juliet home and asked her to reflect on her decision, to mourn or to accept all that was more. Perhaps she was good at knowing the heart of man, Romeo's heart. But did she know *her* heart? If she did, what did she do to honor this knowledge? Displace it with an image of what grief is and what grief does on a theoretical level? Or just sit with it and process it, still? Juliet feared that she would be at a loss for words, if she gave up on the image of her grief and instead rode with hope in the Charioteer's car. What was so terrible about this image? I asked Juliet about it. Her answer pointed to the idea of the right time. She thought about what didn't work in her relationship with Romeo. The timing was off. Either she was too fast and he was too slow, or else he gave her an ultimatum at exactly the wrong time, when the only choice she had was to say, 'fine, do what you must. Ride alone or with someone else.' 'And so I will,' Romeo said, steering his horses into the sunset. But what was fated didn't go away with this ride. Romeo did his thing, dedicating himself to a life without Juliet, and Juliet did her thing, creating art and convincing herself that the source of her inspiration was grief. But the cards here insisted otherwise. The form of Juliet's love was not marked by its loss, but rather by its redemption.

We can think of the Star in the tarot as being a ritualist. If not for the saving grace aspect of it, then why do it at all? Why ritualize what is already a natural act? With the Star we're not with the Pope or the Popess, our clergy in the tarot, reciting prayers, kneeling and drinking wine by the altar. We're with the skyclad goddess here who knows how to draw down the power of celestial light. We're here with the true illuminations of the heart. What did Juliet know about Romeo? The cards also spelled that out. The image of the Charioteer between the two star cards, the Sun and the Star, told us this: 'from here to eternity.' That's what Romeo's drive was all about. Is this a thing of beauty, or are we here with the crushing sublime? It was not for me to decide. This was something Juliet had to think about, as she was the one worried about having the fountain of her creativity dry up. But how could it? Why was there fear in the face of what was already brilliantly plain?

I could have continued with a series of questions whose aim was to probe the perception of what tragedy is, what loss, rage, grief, and regret is, but the cards here in their simplicity gave us enough. When Romeo races in his car towards his Juliet, no death on wheels can catch up with him. If that is good enough for him, it has to be good enough for her, his mirror.

Redemption

Juliet likes to play a game of nothingness with Romeo. She says many things and he says nothing. She decides that there's redemption in Romeo's silence. Since words ruin everything, paying attention to the moves of 'nothing' is more entertaining. 'What nothingness will he now say, tonight?' she likes to ask herself, while casting a string of cards on her table. Displacement by naught.

This is not a game of 'who is to be master,' even though winning is the aim. Sometimes Romeo wins. 'I'm here now,' he says by not saying anything, stressing the idea of 'here.' His favorite line contains 'here' — 'from here to eternity,' he always says to Juliet by not saying anything.

Sometimes Juliet wins. Her winning hand is knowing Romeo's heart. When they both win, they go out at night and look at the stars.

'Give me my Romeo'

THE FIRST TIME I EVER TOOK A DRIVE in a red Corvette was in the US, when I visited a colleague and a friend some 25 years ago. I was on a research semester at Columbia University in New York when Mark C. Taylor, professor of religious studies invited me to his home in Williamstown. He had a house on top of a mountain there. I remember my reaction when I got in his car. I said, 'wow, this is low!' referring to the seats. 'That's the idea,' he said, referring to the benefits of driving in a sports car. 'You want to feel the earth,' he said. 'You want to be as close to it as possible.' I got that, because the more you get to feel the pull of gravity, the more you can appreciate just what kind of flying a good car is capable of. Mark had a thing for the earth as the stuff we all end up with as dead bodies, and wrote a number of books in which he reflects on 'grave matters' – the name of one of his studies on death and cemeteries – and 'speed limits' – the name of another book on where time goes and why we have so little of it left.

But this was all on paper, in theory. Up at his house, Mark's wife was waiting for us. She had a big knife in her hand that she used as a pointer. 'Enter here,' she said, and then went back to orchestrating the dinner in the open kitchen. She was going to serve us beefsteak, house style. I don't recall having tried something in the steak genre that tasted better. I was clearly in the presence of a master. While eating we talked about fear. Mark and I had a philosophical approach to it. His wife was more pragmatic. She told the story about how every time there was a rat invasion, or even just a simple visit from the rodents roaming the earth, Mark would faint. *Every time*, she emphasized. So the man in the red Corvette was not a rat person. He preferred flying to the stars in his car and reaching mountain peaks to the sensation of communing with the creatures of the underworld. And yet one of his favorite pastimes was to trace in charcoal the lines of the gravestones of famous philosophers. He showed me the one he did in Denmark at Søren Kierkegaard's burial place.

As Mark talked about the epitaph and the words about winning at the Christian game inscribed on the stone, his wife demonstrated what she did to the last rat she caught in the kitchen among their silverware. Mark got yellow in his face, and kindly asked her to stop. He was not going to be haunted by that scene again. His wife begged to remind him that since he was passed out, he could not remember what she did. When Werner Herzog shot his Dracula film, he used ten thousand rats. The animal activists were not happy about it, though Herzog stuck to his professional pride. He did not lose a single rat, he told the media, thereby thwarting the rumors that he didn't care. Herzog cared a lot about the rats. They were all stars in his film, the stars of the earth. In *Romeo and Juliet* the woman hands agency to the night. In her address to the forces of the night, she gives us this speech act:

> Give me my Romeo: and, when he shall die,
> Take him and cut him out in little stars,
> And he will make the face of heaven so fine
> That all the world will be in love with night,
> And pay no worship to the garish sun. (3.2)

Juliet here casts a spell by all the rats of the world. She is willing to sacrifice Romeo's body, give it up to the night to chop it up into pieces to be fed to the rats — I assume — in exchange for the night's power to make his body parts sparkle. Then her promise that the whole of humanity will henceforth only worship the night, and forget all about the sun's light. Juliet is playing with some powerful stuff here: 'Give me my Romeo,' she says to the night, 'and I will institute a night order.' Well, her pledge was good, but her timing was off.

In love stories we have vows and we have conjurations. The underlying structure of a vow is the promise of faith. A conjuration operates with the promise of exchange. 'Give me this, and in return for it I will give you that,' the conjuror says, while the other who just makes a vow is oblivious of the transactional economy of faith. When lovers mutually exchange vows, what they don't realize is that they also exchange a potential for conflict. That's why many marriages end up in divorce, and when it gets bad, we hear the parties shout in the courthouses: 'may the rats eat you and all your possessions.'

In a conjure situation the exchange of 'this for that' occurs between the lover and a higher power. The other is not involved. His body or his soul may be used as currency, but there's no mutual transaction here. The lover acts alone.

Let's close this book with this idea, namely the notion that if love is to work on a level that exceeds even the imagination, the lover must always act alone, yet on behalf of the other. If a pact is made, it is not with the lover, but rather with the force that can turn the lover into a myriad of stars. The lover conjuror must be ready to start a whole religion in exchange for the other's brilliance and unique singularity. What is the alternative, really? That they get together and then live happily ever after? How? With a house full of children, cats and dogs, fast cars and not so fast, a mortgage, and a bunch of post-its on the fridge? Why is that interesting? Where is such a life going? Granted, some would say that there's magic in the mundane. But this is not the mundane. The mundane is the ability to go out every night and marvel at the stars. How many couples do that, really? In my own circle of acquaintances, no one ever does that. No one ever lives the mundane life. What most people live is a life of dictations. No one steps into the dark dungeon in order to conjure up the spirits of heaven and hell. *This* would be a mundane act, for the transactions with the sacred in the ordinary life are not about how to sit on the throne of heaven and hell. What would be the purpose of that?

Let us intone instead in magical Juliet's extraordinary language: 'Give me my Romeo, oh wondrous night, and I promise you that when he is back from the land of the dead, we shall both live!'

References & Acknowledgments

CLARK, Stuart (1997). *Thinking with Demons: The Idea of Witchcraft in Early Modern Europe.* Oxford: Clarendon Press.

COPE, Wendy (2008). *Two Cures for Love.* Selected Poems 1979-2006. Faber & Faber.

DICKINSON, Emily (1976). *The Complete Poems of Emily Dickinson.* Ed. Thomas H. Johnson. Back Bay Books

DYLAN, Bob (1963) 'A Hard Rain's a-Gonna Fall' from the album *The Freewheelin' Bob Dylan.* Produced by John Hammond. Released: May 27, 1963.

ELIAS, Camelia (2021). *Read Like the Devil: The Essential Course in Reading the Marseille Tarot.* EyeCorner Press.

——— (2020). *The Power of the Trumps and Pips.* The omnibus edition. EyeCorner Press.

——— (2020). *The Childless Witch: Trembling, Dance, Voice, Oracle, Grace.* EyeCorner Press.

——— (2020). *Tarot Tracings: Essays in Literature and Divination.* EyeCorner Press.

——— (2019). *What is Not: Marseille Tarot à la Carte.* EyeCorner Press.

———— (2019). *Divination with Cards: A Short History*. EyeCorner Press.

———— (2015). *The Oracle Travels Light: Principles of Magic with Cards*. EyeCorner Press.

———— (2014). *Marseille Tarot: Towards the Art of Reading*. EyeCorner Press.

HERZOG, Werner (1972). *Aguirre, the Wrath of God*. Produced by Werner Herzog Filmproduktion, Hessischer Rundfunk. Distributed by Filmverlag der Autoren.

———— (1979). *Nosferatu the Vampyre*. Produced by Werner Herzog Filmproduktion, Gaumont, Zweites Deutsches Fernsehen. Distributed by 20th Century Fox.

———— (1982). *Fitzcarraldo*. Produced by Werner Herzog Filmproduktion, Project Filmproduktion, Filmverlag der Autoren. Distributed by Filmverlag der Autoren (BRD).

———— (2010). *Conquest of the Useless: Reflections from the Making of Fitzcarraldo*. Trans. Krishna Winston. Harper-Collins Books: Ecco.

———— (1999). *Mein liebster Feind – Klaus Kinski*. Produced by Lucki Stipetic.

———— (2014). *Werner Herzog: Interviews*. Ed. Eric Ames. University Press of Mississippi.

———— (2014). *Werner Herzog – A Guide for the Perplexed. Conversations with Paul Cronin*. Faber & Faber.

LELOUCH, Claude (1966). *Un Homme et une Femme*. Produced by Claude Lelouch. Distributed by Allied Artists.

MARION, Jean-Luc (2002). *Prolegomena to Charity*. Trans. Stephen E. Lewis. Fordham University Press.

———— (2007). *The Erotic Phenomenon*. Trans. Stephen E. Lewis. The University of Chicago Press.

SENNA, Ayrton (1993). *Principles of Race Driving*. Hazleton Pub Ltd.

SHAKESPEARE, William (1992). *The Complete Works of William Shakespeare*. Ed. W. J. Craig. London: Magpie Books.

———— (2016). *Romeo and Juliet* (Norton Critical Editions). Ed. Gordon McMullan. W. W. Norton & Company.

SHIKIBU, Murasaki (2002). *The Tale of Genji*. Trans. Royall Tayler. Penguin Classics.

STREISAND, Barbra (1980). 'Woman in Love' from the album *Guilty*. Produced by Barry Gibb, Albhy Galuten, and Karl Richardson.

VASCONCELOS, Luis (2014). 'Pat Symonds remembers Senna: Ayrton moved the goal posts!' Grandprix.com [https://www.grandprix.com/features/feature-pat-symonds-remembers-senna-ayrton-moved-the-goal-posts.html]

TAYLOR, Mark C. (2002) *Grave Matters*. Reaktion Books.

———— (2015). *Speed Limits: Where Time Went and Why We Have So Little Left*. Yale University Press.

TZU, Sun (2003). *The Art of War: Complete Text and Commentaries*. Trans. Thomas Cleary. Shambala Publications.

ACKNOWLEDGMENTS

I AM INDEBTED to the Romeos I am in conversation with in this book in the form of prose poems and personal stories. To inspire to thoughts about infinite love is no small thing. Here I have not merely used the figure of Romeo as a muse, but rather paid tribute to the love that was given to me beyond tropes and the figurative in language games. As nothing was ever asked in return for this love, my devotion goes out to this love, as do my heartfelt thanks.

I also want to thank Werner Herzog for prompting the writing of this book. As he insisted, when such an unusual concoction as this book presents itself, you just ride with the idea and turn your thoughts into a moving picture that moves the heart.

www.ingramcontent.com/pod-product-compliance
Ingram Content Group UK Ltd.
Pitfield, Milton Keynes, MK11 3LW, UK
UKHW040237250426
12048UKWH00040B/1553